P9-DEM-428

HARVEST THE VOTE

HARVEST THE
VOTE

HOW DEMOCRATS CAN WIN AGAIN IN
RURAL AMERICA

JANE KLEEB

ecco

An Imprint of HarperCollins*Publishers*

HarperCollins books may be purchased for educational, business, or sales promotional use. For information, please email the Special Markets Department at SPsales@harpercollins.com.

Ecco® and HarperCollins® are trademarks of HarperCollins Publishers.

FIRST EDITION

DESIGNED BY RENATA DE OLIVEIRA

Library of Congress Cataloging-in-Publication Data has been applied for.

ISBN 978-0-06-296090-0

20 21 22 23 24   LSC   10 9 8 7 6 5 4 3 2 1

To Frank LaMere and Randy Thompson,
who taught me to love the land, respect those
that walked the fields long before us, and listen to
the stories of the people. You both believed
that a mom with a minivan had something
to say and prove.

CONTENTS

HARVEST THE VOTE

PART ONE

THE URBAN-RURAL DIVIDE:
BUILDING THE BRIDGE

INTRODUCTION:
RAISING THE RED FLAG

The eaters and the feeders.

—REVEREND JESSE JACKSON

I n 1985, Reverend Jesse Jackson had the answer to how we bridge the urban and rural divide and showed us all how Democrats can stand with rural voters. He traveled to the small rural town of Chillicothe, Missouri, to stand with farmers in the middle of the farm crisis, a time when a record number of families were losing their farms and the suicide rate among farmers had skyrocketed. As he sat on a tractor, he proclaimed "the eaters and the feeders" needed to unite for real economic and land justice. The land is such a crucial part of our country, our politics, our policy. And yet it's taken for granted, both by politicians and by a large swath of voters. The land connects us all. Even if you have never visited a rural community in your state, we all rely on the food, fiber, and energy created in our small towns across the United States. The weathered hands of a farmer have a lot in common with the calloused hands of a factory worker. Both rural moms and urban moms worry about not being able to get care for her child. The feeling of being left behind and forgotten by our elected officials because big corporations trump the people is a universal feeling among working- and middle-class families no matter where you live.

Rural is a way of life. In our nation's politics, the divide between urban and rural could easily be written off as a problem Democrats should ignore. I have heard many versions of this, from "Ignore the rural areas and go where the people are in the urban centers" to "Why should we give a damn about people voting against their own interests?" and "Rural people are racist and get what they deserve." Then I walk around downtown Hastings, Nebraska, where my husband and I are raising our three daughters, and see a new brewery using local products, a farmers market that would put any Whole Foods to shame, and a boutique that sells all the hip jeans and kids' clothes you would need. I personally know the people who have been forgotten but are still working to keep young people from leaving by building a new library and a main street downtown with green, open spaces. I've been a part of building a playground with all volunteers and know what it meant when over two thousand people stood with the Gaspers family when their son Kevin was killed in Iraq. Our little town of Hastings is consistently pushing back against draconian statewide cuts by raising local taxes to keep the schools and hospital open. The Republican Party takes us "flyover voters" for granted, and the Democratic Party has given up on us.

IT WAS EARLY 2006, AND JEFF HOFFMAN, THE RURAL CAUCUS CHAIR OF THE Young Democrats of America (YDA), called me asking if I would be open to having a young candidate from a rural town speak at our state convention. I was the executive director of YDA and told Jeff no way. I went on to explain that I was sure this candidate, Scott Kleeb, was actually a Republican who could not get out of his party's primary, and there was no way he was going to win anyway. Jeff insisted I take a look at his bio and résumé. When the email arrived, it also included a picture of a tall ranch hand standing in the middle of a vast open field. To say I was smitten is an understatement. That picture got passed around and became my screen saver, and that of many other urban Democrats back then. I called Jeff back and said, "Sure, let's invite Scott to come speak at the convention!"

I even offered to head out to rural Nebraska to provide training on the innovative peer-to-peer young voter program we created in 2004. This was a program that started with the basic premise that when you talk to and engage voters, they vote. Implementing the program led to huge increases in turnout. We tested out lots of messaging and methods of voter contact over several years. But in the end, young people are like all voters. They want to be talked to, they want to be heard, and they want to know that the candidates and the Democratic Party care enough about them to include them in mailings, ads, policies, and messaging. My first trip to Nebraska was planned for later that summer.

Before coming to Nebraska, I had never worked in a rural community. I spent the early years of my career working with AmeriCorps programs in schools, national youth vote projects, and advocacy for eating disorders and mental health care. My career path took me to the great cities of Tallahassee, Washington, D.C., and Philadelphia. When I arrived in the small rural towns that make up Greater Nebraska in June 2006, I was instantly struck by how everyone said hello, raised a finger in a silent wave when you met them on the road (not the middle finger!), and communicated an overall sense of looking out for one another. I quickly saw that my assumptions about Scott were wrong. He was running a strong race and was gaining on his Republican opponent in the polls. He did this by running a positive campaign. Surprisingly, he did it while projecting a progressive vision in a district that is mostly farm and ranch country. When Scott spoke, he never talked down or dumbed down the complicated issues facing rural Nebraska. He challenged all those he spoke with to punch above their weight and encouraged them to become part of a growing group of people with a common desire to help build rural America. Scott believed in the rural voters of Nebraska just as much as they believed in him. While Scott did not win his race, he came closer to doing so in that district than any Democrat had done in over fifty years.

On our first date, Scott grabbed a six-pack of beer and "cake" for the cows as we headed out to his pickup truck. Scott was working as a ranch hand on the McGinn Ranch, his cousin's operation, outside the small Sandhills town of Dunning, an area with many more cattle than people. We drove to the top of one of the highest hills in the area, from which we could watch the birds, deer, and cows on the prairie below us. Blades of grass danced in the wind like an ocean around his truck. As I learned to feed cattle the "cake" (little morsels of goodness consisting of alfalfa and molasses), I began to understand the deep love family ranchers have for their livestock. In fact, on many family ranches, the cows often have names, and the rancher can point out to you the "good mamas" and those who might "give you a run for your money." The way ranchers and farmers treat their livestock and land is something I get defensive about when I see a tweet or blog post on how eating meat is animal cruelty. There's no question industrial agriculture hurts animals, workers, and our environment, but I have never met a family farmer or rancher who would not walk straight into a blizzard to save their animals or to help their neighbors.

The sunset colors filled the sky and we sat there in Scott's truck listening to music and the soft lowing of cattle all around us. Over lots of dates just like this one, including the time I tumbled into a patch of burs because I had no idea how to drive a four-wheeler, I fell in love with both the Sandhills and rural Nebraska. What roped me in was the way the stars fill the night sky, the teasing of the local bartender as I order the proper Nebraska drink, red beer (this is beer mixed with tomato juice—try it, you'll find it life changing!), and the way in which everyone in town is part of the ranching community—whether it's the employees at the feedstore, the local vet, the town banker, teachers in the school, or the ranchers themselves. Small rural towns have a shared spirit of "We're all in this to-gether." I first fell in love with the Sandhills, but to the likely chagrin of many of the Republicans who run the state, Scott and I also fell in love, married, and chose rural Nebraska as our home.

Most of my background would make it seem un-likely that I could write a book about rural voters. I grew up in Plantation, Florida, a town outside Fort Lauderdale. I therefore did not grow up in a rural community. I had never lived on a farm or ranch. Scott and I are raising our three girls in Hastings, a town of about 25,000 people in the south central part of Nebraska, a town best known as the birthplace of Kool-Aid. We are also restoring a 140-year-old farm just outside the small town of Ayr, a grand little town of eighty wonderful people. Scott is in the cattle business with the Morgan family, selling beef across the world. I am the chair of the Nebraska Democratic Party and run a grassroots nonprofit group, Bold Nebraska. I have spent the last decade traveling to rural communities in Nebraska, Minnesota, Oklahoma, Texas, Virgina, West Virginia, Oregon, and South Dakota, all with the goal of working with landowners and tribal nations to stop pipelines from taking the land, polluting our water, and adding to the real problems of climate change.

I was, like many in rural communities, raised in a Republican, pro-life family. However, the Republican Party that my family so identified with is unrecognizable today. At my core—indeed, at the core of all the rural people I meet and love—is a desire, more than anything, to have our country work for everyone, not just for a few people at the top. A deep sense of fairness is at the core of America's rural communities. Progressive and populist roots run deep in rural communities. When immigrants moved out west, the first institutions they built were schools and churches. They saw education, community, and family as pivotal to building their towns and futures. While people who pushed for reforms and resisted the troubled status quo in the cities called themselves progressives, rural people who pushed back against entrenched interests, like the big banks that were trying to crush them, considered themselves populists. These are two sides of the same coin. President Trump and the white nationalist movement have attempted to co-opt the word *populist*, but history shows us populist and progressive roots are part of the same tree of reform. I largely stay away from these two labels because they carry with them perceptions you'd need an entire series of books to dig into. Rarely do I meet someone in rural America who describes himself or herself as a populist or a progressive. You are more likely to hear people describe themselves by the sports team they follow or church they belong to.

The land is everything to rural people. We belong to the land. Livelihoods are tied to the land. Tradition and culture is wrapped up in the land. We protect the land that was first nourished by our Native American brothers and sisters. We are stewards of the land. We have the land and the land has us. Understanding our ties to the land is the first step in understanding how to connect and stand with us. Democrats need to stand up for rural people when they are hurting, when their land is being threatened, and when they see a two-hundred-year flood every twenty-five years. The Republican Party and President Trump will take the stage saying "I love the farmers," and then pass policies that cripple farmers: unnecessary trade wars and tariffs, eminent domain, and tax breaks for huge corporations and mega-farms.

The Democratic Party has largely abandoned rural communities. Rarely in our history have we reached out and brought rural interests to the policy table of our party. Notable exceptions can be found in the 1930s and '40s, when, under FDR, Democrats got behind several farm programs to include the Agricultural Adjustment Act and, most especially, the Rural Electrification Act. It was under the REA, of course, that electricity was brought to rural counties and small towns all across America. A more recent but no less notable exception was during the 1980s, when Democrats stepped up to help rural America during the farm credit crisis, a crisis that brought farmers to D.C. on their tractors and also brought Willie Nelson's historic Farm Aid drive. That drive highlighted the massive losses of family-run farms and efforts to keep families on the land. With those few exceptions, it's hard to point to any other time in our history when we, as a party, have embraced rural issues or even taken rural voters seriously. Some Democrats, in fact, sneer at rural residents, labeling them "gun lovers" and "racists." We've all probably heard some version of "Who needs 'em? They're all dying off anyway."

Rural people deserve better from *all* politicians. I'm tired of Republican politicians who constantly use hot-button wedge issues to keep rural and urban voters divided. I'm tired, too, of Democrats sitting on the sidelines, allowing this to happen and not working to fix the problem. Many people, when they think about rural America, if they think about it at all, conjure up images of poorly educated white people with racist attitudes. But after living and working in a rural area for nearly fifteen years, I know that's not the case. When I think of rural America, I think of the lights of tractors moving through the fields at night still harvesting the crops we use for fuel, fiber, and food. I think of old-timers with hands as weathered as their boots helping to brand calves in the spring and fix their neighbors' fence in the fall. I think of young people revitalizing the main streets of small towns with farm-to-table restaurants and craft microbreweries. I think of the beauty of the Sandhills and the awesome sight of countless stars in the night sky undimmed by the glare of city lights. I think of barns and community centers filled with the music of country bands or, at other times, with Mexican music accompanied by the wide swirl of colorful dresses. I think of families coming together to share meals, laughter, and stories. I think of the parents in these families doing their best to raise their children in "the good life" and working hard to preserve for them a legacy that's worth passing down. On the one hand, rural people are fiercely independent, and on the other, they display a fierce sense of community, a reliance on one another to fix fence and brand cattle. It's why I love rural America.

I DROVE UP TO THE SANDHILLS FOR A MEETING WITH LANDOWNERS WHO HAD concerns about balancing wind farms and property rights. Walking into the room, I noticed it was filled with lots of boots and cowboy hats, so I knew I was in the right place. An old-timer came up to me, gave me a slight smile, and said, "So you are Jane Kleeb. I thought you would have horns and a tail." I laughed, patting my head and checking behind me to see if I somehow missed the devil's tail. "Nope, no horns or tail. I'm just here to listen to your concerns." I showed up and listened to what rural voters are interested in and concerned about, which is what Democrats need to do more of in rural communities. We need to stop saying "Rural people are voting against their interests" and start showing up to actually learn what those interests are. We can no longer ignore, write off, and dismiss rural America. We must invest real money and significant time to win again in our small towns. We must stand up and say we are not going to let the politics of the past define how we organize in the future. When we are tired of the same old story of how rural people are portrayed and instead listen to the people who live there, whether at the seed store or in the hospital or grocery store, the tables will begin to turn and we the people can be at the center of our politics once again.

The Democratic Party desperately needs rural voters. We need them not simply to win elections, although obviously I want to see that happen. The Democratic Party needs rural voters because they are part of the American fabric; they can contribute ideas and solutions that will help us confront the many issues facing our country today. Climate change, education, health care, immigration, technology, jobs, and of course food and agricultural policies are all issues of tremendous concern to rural voters. These are issues that, by and large, are also important to the Democratic Party, regardless of where you live. Most of us want these concerns dealt with. We also want our democratic processes to be open and fair. We want our children to have a decent shot at having a life equal to or better than our own. In doing all of this, we need to create authentic relationships with all our constituencies and, through them, create solutions that restore common sense and decency to our body politic.

It is true our rural communities are facing a decline in the number of people living and working in them. This can change with the help of policies that enable more families to put down roots in towns where the cost of living is affordable and the doors are open to entrepreneurs and the new pioneers—those who bring clean energy, tech jobs, and brilliant ideas to our small towns—welcoming them to live alongside our family farmers and ranchers, who are the backbone of our rural communities. Families choose to live in rural communities for the way of life and the open space. Families choose to live in rural communities to carry on the farm or ranch or local hardware store. More and more immigrants and new Americans are calling rural communities their home because of jobs and great schools.

The Democratic Party can and should be the ones standing up for the little guy. It is who we are as a party. Rural people want the government to help families, not make a few people at the top richer. Democrats living on the coasts share many of the same goals as rural Democrats and Independents—break up big banks, stop the mega-mergers, protect workers, expand public education, make health care affordable, and confront climate change. We share the core value of fairness. Red states have passed progressive ballot campaigns from medical marijuana to marriage equality to Medicaid expansion. And yet it's too rare when Democrats at the federal and statewide level win in rural states. Though there were a few bright spots in the 2018 cycle: Laura Kelly of Kansas and Tony Evers of Wisconsin winning governorships; Xochitl Torres Small of New Mexico and Abby Finkenauer of Iowa winning House seats; Nikki Fried becoming agriculture commissioner of Florida, the only statewide elected Democrat. It's more likely that rural Democrats win at the local level where you can create change faster. In fact, in Nebraska we had 850 Democrats run, and 73 percent of them won their elections. None of those were statewide, and none were for federal office.

So how does a girl who grew up in South Florida and lived in D.C. now feel competent to write a book about how the Democratic Party needs to reach rural voters? To take a lesson from Michelle Obama, "It doesn't go away, that feeling that you shouldn't take me that seriously. What do I know? I share that with you because we all have doubts in our abilities, about our power and what that power is." I remember what Mrs. Barbara James, the principal of Bond Elementary in Tallahassee, where I ran an AmeriCorps program, once told me. I went to her on the first day nervous about being a white girl from Fort Lauderdale in the predominantly African American community. I did not want people in the community to think I was some do-gooder outsider. I wanted to be part of the school and be there for the kids. She looked at me and said, "You are standing here. That's all that matters."

I no longer doubt what I bring to the table. I learned a ton of lessons working shoulder to shoulder with farmers, ranchers, and Native Americans in rural communities. When we started the fight against the Keystone XL Pipeline, or when we set out to help pass the Affordable Care Act, I did not know all the details of these two policy areas. In fact, I started out largely ignorant on both fronts. That all began to change when I walked into church basements, sale barns, diners, and bars with two open ears and one closed mouth. I listened to people who did know something about these issues and worked hard to earn their trust. Then in turn I asked them to become activists and advocates, something not one single farmer or rancher saw in any of their futures, especially not alongside a Democrat. We set out on a journey together to help ourselves and our neighbors build a future for our kids and communities.

As a leader in the Democratic Party, I am waving a giant red flag in hopes of getting your attention. If we want rural communities to vote for Democrats, thereby making not just our party but our nation stronger, then we have to start showing them we give a damn again. As Democrats, we simply have not offered another choice to rural voters. We have not shown up to listen to the issues they care about. We have not looked to rural people for ideas. We have not invested in rural candidates. We abandoned state parties, the backbone of all elections, in rural states. Democrats everywhere must work to understand rural America a little bit better and to feel an urgency to connect with them a lot more.

What I hope to achieve in this book is to show that there is more that unites us than divides us. That when we welcome all shades of blue at our big Democratic table, we are stronger. I do not pretend to speak for all rural Americans. Every state has rural communities, and the regional differences across our huge country are real. There is a common culture among rural people, but the towns of the rural South look and sound much different from the rural areas of the Plains states. I certainly do not have all the answers, and one book is not going to solve a generational divide rendered by deep mistrust of a party rural residents have not seen or heard from in decades. I've been a Democratic Party activist for years, but before moving to a rural town myself, I made the same mistakes I see happening now. We have to focus on the issues that spur people to political action and start to explain how the Democratic Party can begin the hard work of winning back (yes, *back*, because we used to win here consistently) rural voters. Without rural voters, our party and our country will never reach full potential.

1

FROM THE TRACTOR BRIGADE TO THE TRACTOR CAUCUS OF ONE

Showing up is the foundation to building the house. If you don't start there, you are screwed. If you are an attorney from Manhattan, then don't pretend you are a backhoe operator from Indiana. Don't change who you are, just come to where we are.

—SENATOR JON TESTER,
THE ONLY WORKING FARMER IN THE U.S. SENATE

Jim Hightower, the two-term, Wrangler-wearing agriculture commissioner from Texas, has always been a progressive populist and bristles at the thought that Trump has redefined that word. For Jim, and many in rural communities, politics is not about "right to left, but top to bottom." Big banks and big corporations have been stepping all over working families for decades; we have movies and libraries filled with these stories. The difference these days is Republicans keep talking to rural communities, pretending they are the ones who will turn things around while using wedge issues to keep us divided. Democrats have stopped showing up in rural communities, so we've lost touch with what matters most to rural folks. It was not always this way. The Pew Research Center, a nonprofit that tracks political trends, lays it out in stark truths. Just twenty years ago, rural communities were split evenly between both parties and education was the top issue for both Democrats and Republicans. Today, the top issue for Republicans is terrorism, and for Democrats it is health care. None of the top five issues are the same on either side of the aisle. We are talking past each other. I am not putting on rose-colored glasses and hoping for days long gone. As Democrats, we now have to reconnect with the land and chart a new path with unlikely alliances if we are to turn around the losses.

The Democratic Party has a long tradition of standing with working families, whether that is family farmers or union workers. In the 1920s and '30s, family farmers were hit by low crop prices and our country was reeling from a major war. Franklin Delano Roosevelt's New Deal generated programs like the Rural Electrification Act, which brought electricity and jobs to rural America, and the Shelterbelt Project, which planted trees to protect the soil from erosion and to lift up family farmers. The government and elected officials were there for the people. Democrats showed up and were elected from rural communities to bring rural voices into our country's policies and politics. The Democratic Party of today, however, has lost this relationship and is missing out on strong, creative, entrepreneurial rural voices in all aspects of our body politic.

In our more recent history, the moment that high-lights rural communities rising up against big corporations and fighting for economic fairness, with urban allies right at their side, is the farm crisis of the 1980s. Democratic leaders like Jesse Jackson and black pastors traveled to rural towns to engage in civil disobedience and rallies to bring attention to the crisis at hand. Farms were being auctioned off as families, after generations of ranching and farming, could no longer afford to live and work the land. The drop in crop exports, because of the U.S. grain embargo against the Soviet Union, kicked off the farm crisis. Crop prices were lower than the cost of production. Oil prices were high. Family farmers and ranchers were taking on more debt to purchase modern equipment that could manage the larger operations they now needed to take on in order to make a profit. Gone were the days that a family could make it with 160 acres. A farming family needed at least 800 acres to turn a profit, the equivalent of roughly 1,600 acres today. To put that in context, it's about 1,600 football fields, or roughly two Central Parks. Family farmers and ranchers were committing suicide at alarming rates. It was a crisis pure and simple.

During a cold and rainy February in 1979, farm families got on their tractors and rode over 1,200 miles to our nation's capital. The tractors stayed on the national mall for over three months to get the attention of our country's leaders. Hand-painted signs on the tractors read FARMS, NOT ARMS and SAVE THE FAMILY FARM. This became known as the Tractor Brigade. It was a moment that created activists who are still going strong today like John Hansen, a family farmer and president of the Nebraska Farmers Union, who is now helping build solar and wind farms all across the Plains states as he pushes state governments to support regenerative agricultural practices that keep the soil healthy. John remembers going to meetings of the American Agriculture Movement and the Farmers Union, listening to the stories of families trying to get economic justice and security of markets for the food they were producing. John sees the loss of confidence in politics by rural people and has to battle on a daily basis the Nebraska state legislature as they continually try to give big corporations major handouts while leaving property tax relief on the cutting room floor, "As our state's family farmers and ranchers are being forced out of business, their legislature wants to stab them in the back with a corporate pitchfork." The stories John heard in the eighties were no different from what he hears today, with the very notable exception being there are far fewer family farmers these days and even fewer politicians who truly understand and stand with them. When John reflects on writing plenty of speeches for Democratic presidential candidates and sitting in rooms consulting with the party on how to reach rural voters, he gets right to the point: "The Democratic Party might talk about rural issues here and there, but farmers do not see them following through on the words. So if you are going to vote on economic issues, which rural people have and could do again, then you need to know the candidates and the party are going to take action. Democrats when in office fall back to supporting Big Ag and trade policies that hurt family farmers and ranchers. In the end, if voters think both parties are the same in actual economic policies for rural America, they are going to vote for the party that supports some of the cultural issues as their fallback. It might not be right, but this is what is happening." The platform and values of Democrats are better for rural America, but if you get forgotten once someone is in office, you do not vote for that party again.

Learning about what Democrats did back then is instructive for what we can be doing now. Look at Jackson's visit to Missouri in 1985. He told a crowd of farmers and ranchers protesting the farm closures in Missouri that it was time for the "the eaters and the feeders, black and white, to unite for justice in rural America. We have the resources to declare a state of emergency, a moratorium on farm foreclosures, and to loan farmers money to plant this season." Jackson understood the land and farming. He knew African American families owned farms of their own before moving to cities, and he recognized the historical and economic ties he was lifting up. He also knew plenty of black families were (and are!) still farming. Jackson was a prominent Democrat who used his platform to give a boost to rural people's voices at a time when they needed a champion.

The farm crisis also gave us the longest-running benefit concert and the one time every single year that rural people are celebrated—Farm Aid. In 1985, Willie Nelson, Neil Young, John Mellencamp, and later Dave Matthews all joined forces to save the family farmer. Literally. Willie Nelson did not start Farm Aid to be political in the partisan sense of the word. He started Farm Aid because he saw people hurting and knew his huge megaphone could help families. Using culture and music reached people in a truly unique way and brought new voices to the table.

Speaking in an Iowa public television documentary on the farm crisis, Willie explained why he started Farm Aid: "I was glad we were there to give them a voice. One of the best things to happen was getting us all together talking about it. I knew if we could give these farmers a voice, then that would help them, and that's what we've been trying to do."

Willie often jokes his music brings together the hippies and the rednecks. He told *Parade* magazine back in 2010 that his music "gives people a chance to enjoy something together" and to "find out they have things in common and don't really hate each other." There is something profound about this simple and straightforward view on how his music brought people together despite their backgrounds or outward appearance. Stereotypes begin to melt away and you start to truly see people. I've been to several Farm Aids. By early evening, the guy in bib overalls is high-fiving the biker and getting a beer with a tree hugger, and all of them are there to support family farmers and ranchers. We need more of this in America. The Democratic Party needs to focus more on bridging the urban and rural divide. Obviously we are not going to agree on all issues. We can find those places where we can help families, especially family farmers and ranchers who are producing our food and fiber and are now also growing the clean energy to confront the issue of climate change, a crisis many of us care about and one that is critical to address given the vast areas of everyday life that looming crisis touches.

Because of Farm Aid, you started to see the Farm Bill of 1985 get more feedback from actual family farmers as people organized their own bill-writing sessions to get a law that helped them, not big corporations. Democrats and cultural icons like Willie Nelson were standing with family farmers, while President Ronald Reagan vetoed packages to help rural America, essentially spitting in the faces of those farmers who rode their tractors to try and be noticed. Reagan said the bill was "a massive new bailout that would add billions to the deficit," and he maintained that the government could not "bail out every farmer hopelessly in debt." That is harsh. And that is coming from an icon of the Republican Party.

Senator Tom Harkin of Iowa was there, speaking to farmers' concerns, making it clear they may have voted for Ronald Reagan, but as a Democrat he was there to stand with them. Reflecting on his work years later, Harkin said farmers "needed a champion on the front lines for them. They needed to know someone was hearing their pleas. I felt this is hurting good, solid farmers and an entire generation of young farmers." Harkin was not alone. Nebraska was represented by two Democratic senators, Edward Zorinsky and J. James Exon, at this time. The Senate elections in 1986, right in the middle of the farm crisis, flipped a historic amount of red to blue seats in rural states like North Dakota, South Dakota, Alabama, and Georgia. Democratic leaders stood together with farmers pushing back hard against the Republican Party and Ronald Reagan.

Rural communities today are in a state of crisis similar to the one in the 1980s. The suicide rate today among farmers is actually almost 50 percent higher than it was in the 1980s, and in some studies higher than war veterans, a sign many in the agriculture community say is a major indicator that another farm crisis is headed our way or is here already. Access to mental health continues to be a huge challenge in rural America, and this was one of the red flags during the 1980s farm crisis that got people's attention. And yet farmers today are being ignored and forgotten by the Democratic Party. One of the answers as to why is pretty simple—the Tractor Brigade has shrunk down to a Tractor Caucus of One. Senator Jon Tester of Montana is the only member of the U.S. Senate that still gets dirt under his fingernails when he goes back home to his family farm. When you talk to Senator Tester, it is exactly the same as talking to any farmer or rancher leaning up against the pickup truck. There is no filter. There is no checking in with a pollster on how to say something. Tester is authentic and cares deeply about rural America. Rural Americans are not images on a poster—they are his friends and family. He has not given up on the possibility that the Democratic Party can learn lessons from the years of losses. Tester wants Democrats to win again because he knows we are the party of the people looking out for the little guy. He sincerely believes the only way we will win again is if we truly hear rural people and start solving the big issues facing our country together—whether you ride a tractor, a bus, or the subway or call an Uber.

I got to talk to Tester for this book. I wanted to get his

perspective on how he succeeds as a farmer-legislator. His advice is simple and to the point, just as that of a farmer would be. He sums up how Democrats need to reach rural people: "Show up and listen." He chuckles and then says, "You actually get smarter when you listen to rural people." Both Senator Tester and I agree that to reach rural America again, we are going to have to do more than showing up and listening; we need to talk about issues beyond access to broadband, which is the typical go-to issue urban people bring up when talking about rural America. We need to understand that the issues of many rural folks overlap with the issues that drive the Democratic Party writ large.

Candidates and the larger Democratic Party do not have to twist themselves into a pretzel on hot-button issues and they do not have to throw on camo pants and a Carhartt jacket to speak with rural families. The Democratic values of hard work, looking out for one another, and above all else fairness are all part of the fabric of rural communities and those matter to urban communities, too. Senator Tester hit the nail on the head: "Showing up is the foundation to building the house. If you don't start there, you are screwed. If you are an attorney from Manhattan, then don't pretend you are a backhoe operator from Indiana. Don't change who you are, just come to where we are. The Democrats failed to do this in the last several election cycles. They just did not show up."

Senator Tester told me about all the times a member of Congress from an urban area would tell him how rural people should think and what their issues are, when Tester knew full well that person's feet had not touched rural land. Urban elected officials at times exhibit an air of arrogance, assuming they know better what is best for us in rural communities. I am not even sure they realize they are being so dismissive, especially when they say things like "Don't they realize they are voting against their best interests?" Tester got right to that point: "Rural Americans' concerns are real, and they care about some of the same issues as urban people do, like infrastructure, health care, and education. They talk about them differently. Take climate change, for example. Of course climate change is a huge problem facing rural America. If you come into rural America and say you are going to regulate carbon-based fuels, you are screwed in rural America. You know why? Because a farmer pulls up to put diesel in their tractor every morning. They don't have options right now beyond that for the tractor. So you better figure out a better way to talk about this issue, like how farms can help solve the problem of too much carbon dioxide in the air and how policies can help family-run food production. Let's talk about options and how farmers can help solve the problem."

Even though Senator Tester is easygoing, you can hear the frustration in his voice. After all, he represents the Tractor Caucus of One. I am sure that what he is telling me he has said a million times to Democratic Caucus leaders, donors, and rooms of activists, without much effect on the party message or party resource allocation to rural states. "Let me be honest, Democrats did not show up last time. Republicans did not do any better. All they talk about is taking away taxes and regulations, and we all know rural people care about a lot more. Rural America is smarter and deserves a lot better. People smell phoniness from a mile away. Politicians try to figure out what people want to hear and then say that rather than standing up for their values and listening to people. We are a big country, and diversity is what makes us great and gives us strength. So when you hear people saying we need to ignore rural America, we just can't do that. I get frustrated with people who supported Trump because he is a train wreck. On the other hand, I get it. They did not do it because he is a grifter, which he is; they voted for him because they thought he was the better choice. The party did not do a good enough job pushing back on the lies and crap the Republicans were putting out on Hillary Clinton, and she was just nowhere to be found in rural communities. Trump is a foreign concept to people out here and yet they still voted for him because the Democrats were nowhere to be found and they were not talking about the issues important to rural America. I try to tell leaders all the time, please do not talk about forty-seven issues—just come up with five and stick to those."

I could hear ringing in the background and knew it meant Senator Tester was getting called to the floor for a vote. He paused and said, with a strong sense of purpose, "I honestly think Hillary thought she was going to win. I thought she was going to win. There is a big lesson there to be learned. I have been through three rip-your-face-off campaigns and there was never one moment in time I thought I was going to win. I found out the night of the election I was going to win, once the people had spoken. Democrats just did not show up out here. We don't need Democrats to stand up and tell us what they think our issues are, we need Democrats to listen to us again and find out what is important to rural people. Not what you think is important to them."

DURING THE FARM CRISIS, RANCHERS AND FARMERS FELT ISOLATED AND FORgotten as the big banks came knocking, illegally in many cases, to foreclose on their family operations. In those days, America rose up and stood by their side. Giving rural people the space and platform to lead, Democratic leaders and allies focused on the crisis at hand until resources were found and bills written to help people. Now, family farmers are once more feeling isolated and forgotten, with industrial agriculture and the producers of fossil fuels closing in on them and either taking land away from them by eminent domain or polluting it so much the land becomes worthless.

Democrats were there for rural communities, but since the 1980s, when was the last time you heard the Democratic Party pushing policies like country-of-origin labeling and the right to repair—a policy that would allow farmers to fix their tractors rather than traveling to an "authorized" dealer—to address everyday issues facing rural communities? Where is the Democratic Party as family land across rural America is being taken away by eminent domain for the private gain of fossil fuel corporations? Where are the programs to help rural schools that are being consolidated, forcing kids to sit on buses for an hour or more? Where is the Democratic Party on helping solve food deserts in rural towns, where the local Casey's General Store is the only place within thirty minutes to buy milk? Where are the programs to help entrepreneurs as they open up craft breweries, ecotourism businesses, and boutiques so Walmart isn't our only option for clothing?

When you don't have the voices and faces of rural communities in the room, bringing the issues they are facing to the table and the ideas they have to solve the big problems of climate change and health care, then you get what we are seeing right now—a party that focuses most of its resources on the coasts and a handful of "swing states" in order to win elections because they assume the red and rural ones are too hard to win. No one is in the room to explain otherwise. As Democrats, we cannot have a Tractor Caucus of One. We need a whole fleet representing the regional and racial diversity of rural communities across our country in order for us to truly connect with rural voters again.

We've done it before. The Democratic Party used to be full of representatives from rural states. Senators Kent Conrad and Byron Dorgan represented North Dakota together for decades, same for Senators Tim Johnson and Tom Daschle of South Dakota. Senators Ben Nelson and Bob Kerrey were both governors and senators in Nebraska. Senators Max Cleland and Sam Nunn served Georgia. Senator Mark Pryor and President Bill Clinton were both from Arkansas. Senator Tom Harkin of Iowa was a strong Democrat who led on rural issues for decades. More recently we had Senator Claire McCaskill from Missouri and Heidi Heitkamp of North Dakota. There were scores of governors and House members, too. The muscles we had in rural America have long since atrophied. But it doesn't need to be this way. We can win again. We just need to listen and find the common ground. And there's plenty of common ground.

2

THE UNLIKELY ALLIANCE

We are among those with the most to lose and the least to gain from Keystone XL Pipeline. The question is this to President Obama: Is he raising the heavy hand of Big Oil or is he going to raise the hand and the spirits of the American people?

—RANDY THOMPSON, NEBRASKA CATTLEMAN

One way to bridge the urban-rural divide is to tell stories of how and where it's already happening. One of the biggest environmental battles in decades, the fight over the Keystone XL Pipeline, is one of those stories. Rural farmers, ranchers, Native nations, and urban climate advocates all came together to take on Big Oil, the Canadian government, the Republican Party, and even significant leaders within the Democratic Party. Bringing these diverse elements together was not easy. Key lessons of our fight include national and local groups working hand in hand and all of us engaging in constant actions, rooted in a strong sense of place, that built trust among everyone. The large national environmental organizations worked alongside the small but mighty groups on the ground. Foundations that normally only gave to the big environmental groups started to fund grassroots and frontline groups all along the pipeline route. This was a major shift from previous campaigns when only large and "proven groups" were given funding. We created a shared strategy that included rural ideas and voices from the front lines at the heart of our national message. We never shied away from looking powerful politicians in the eye, including President Obama, and telling them they had a choice: Stand with the people or with Big Oil. At the core of our fight was a strong belief in the local pipeline fighters and water protectors, since they had the most to lose. In the end, we won what was truly a David versus Goliath battle.

It was early 2009. I had finished a stint as a reporter for MTV during the 2008 campaign and was now getting more active in Nebraska local politics. I led the Service Employees International Union's Change That Works project in our state, which was working to pass health care and union reforms in the first hundred days of President Obama's first term in office. Our task was to convince Ben Nelson, our Democratic senator at the time, to vote for the Affordable Care Act (Obamacare) at a time when the Tea Party was on the rise. After traveling the state nonstop and seeing up close and personal how many issues rural and urban Nebraskans shared, in the end, Nelson voted in favor of Obamacare. However, it passed with a clause that was used by Republicans to vilify Senator Nelson. The Cornhusker Kickback, as it became known, was a part of the Affordable Care Act that simply made it clear in the law that states could expand Medicaid. After carrying out two years of grassroots organizing and providing all the resources we needed, the Democratic Party and all the other national allies pulled up stakes and left. They had gotten what they wanted—Obamacare passed—and they left all of us here to pick up the pieces. At the end of 2011, Ben Nelson announced he wouldn't run for reelection and Democrats lost the seat in 2012 even as President Obama won his second term.

I figured it would be another decade before a big issue would come up where the national organizations would need Nebraska again, so in 2010 after we passed Obamacare, I turned to a local donor, Dick Holland. We sat in his living room and decided we needed a group to take on "the politics of mean," as Dick characterized what was happening in our state. A group not tied to the Democratic Party, who in our state at the time was not interested in reformers. We needed a group that would continue the urban-rural bridge building Change That Works started. A group not scared to punch back. That afternoon, we decided to start Bold Nebraska and set out with the single goal of transforming Nebraska's political landscape with everyone at the table. And we meant everyone—farmers, the creative class, hunters, small-business owners, moms, college students, and activists from Omaha to Scottsbluff.

As all this was happening in Nebraska, another drama was playing out in Alberta, Canada, which would intersect with my work, and my life, in a fateful way. One of the most destructive projects on earth, the tar sands in Alberta, was expanding recklessly. Most Americans had never heard of the tar sands, but in Canada it was becoming a highly controversial topic, as the industry was a major contributor to deforestation, toxic contamination, violation of indigenous rights, land grabs, and climate change. First Nations, the indigenous people of Canada, knew firsthand the risks to their land and water and were trying hard to explain it to anyone who would listen. At that time, the industry was planning to expand its production of two million barrels a day to as much as ten million barrels a day. Their plans also included adding at least six additional maximum-capacity pipelines that would crisscross the United States to get their product to the export market, mostly to China. The mining of tar sands releases far more carbon into the atmosphere than any other form of fossil fuel extraction. It furthermore requires the cutting down of the boreal forest, a huge natural sink for the sequestration of carbon. Once the tar sands have been mined, what's left behind is mile after mile of large, deep pits filled with polluted, toxic water. Part of Canada's expansion plan was the building of the massive Keystone XL Pipeline, which would carry tar sands through the heartland of America to the Gulf Coast, thereby putting at risk both the environmentally sensitive Nebraska Sandhills and the largest body of underground freshwater in America, the Ogallala Aquifer.

In late 2008, a small group of environmental funders and organizations met to discuss stopping the tar sands. No major environmental groups were making the tar sands a signature issue yet (the national groups truly supported the local groups as the campaign developed; more on that soon). The major environmental groups were mostly focused on the cap-and-trade bill making its way through Congress, a promise President Obama made on the trail he would pass. The bill ended up failing and was considered one of the biggest setbacks in environmental movement history.

John Broder of *The New York Times* wrote a reflective piece on the demise of cap and trade, summing it up in a sentence: "Why did cap and trade die? The short answer is that it was done in by the weak economy, the Wall Street meltdown, determined industry opposition and its own complexity."

Here's the longer answer. At the time cap and trade failed, the climate change movement and the environmental movement at large were centered on the coasts.

Rural America was not in the mix. Farmers, ranchers, fisher folk, and communities of color who live in rural communities and work in jobs tied to the land and water that already face the impacts of climate change were left out. The fight to pass this bill was centered on the traditional lobbying of Washington, D.C.—legislators in their offices or at fancy dinners and fundraisers in large urban areas. All of the resources were spent in the halls of Congress instead of on the streets and fields of America. Ironically, it's in the fields and fishing waters of rural America where climate change will likely have its greatest impact on the lives and livelihoods of our nation's citizens, on our national security and food supply.

The hearts, minds, and attention of the public at large were not brought into the process of trying to pass the cap-and-trade bill. The "big greens," a shorthand term for the national environmental organizations, were not fighting alongside the largest potential fighting force of all—the actual citizens living and working in rural communities, who faced a direct threat of losing their land and water to pipelines and the fracking boom. The great tragedy of this massive oversight by the big green leaders is that the interest was obviously there, in that some of these rural communities were already, on their own, beginning to take on the oil industry in budding fights against both fracking and pipelines. Josh Fox was working with landowners in his own backyard to stop fracking in Pennsylvania, which led to the award-winning documentary *Gasland*. Josh was a trailblazer in organizing neighbors and citizens across the United States that no one was listening to as their water became polluted while the fracked gas industry pretended gas was better than coal or oil. Activists in New York, led by Jay Halfon, were meeting at kitchen tables to figure out how they could pressure Democrats to listen to their real concerns of water pollution and land grabs they saw happening in their backyards. The NIMBY (not in my backyard) crowd had not yet met up with the KING (keep it in the ground) crowd. This was all about to change.

Let's get back to the 2008 meeting of environmental leaders and funders who called themselves the Tar Sands Campaign. TransCanada officially applied to the United States for the Keystone XL permit in September 2008. The small group discussed the far-fetched idea to stop the tar sands massive expansion plans by targeting the Keystone XL Pipeline in the United States rather than in Canada. The pitchman for the idea was Kenny Bruno, a fast-talking, hard-driving New Yorker who worked in the smallest corners of the world to stop climate change and had even hung from bridges with Greenpeace to make his point. They were influenced in part by an analysis done by Paul Blackburn, then a lawyer with Plains Justice and later a key analyst and advisor for us, who argued that because the industry needed relatively few pipelines for expansion, it was more strategic than focusing on mines, refineries, or corporate customers. Being from the Midwest, Paul also thought the pipeline fights would galvanize a new crop of activists—farmers and ranchers. Bruno made the case that the power of environmental groups should be focused on stopping the expanded development of North American tar sands, and, critically, they needed to throw out the old playbook of only focusing on the halls of Congress.

Kenny Bruno has many stories of trying to convince powerful environmental leaders to change the way they organized campaigns. I remember one story he told me when leaders met to discuss the Keystone XL work and at one point in the meeting, a powerful leader of a national group grabbed his notebook and stormed out of the room, saying as he left, "This is stupid and will never work." Interestingly, the younger staffers from that same group stayed. They got it. They were seeing the fracktivists and young people getting very impatient with the lack of climate action. I was not in the room that day. In fact, although I was aware that climate change was an issue, the extent of my activism at that point was getting my kids to recycle. I had no understanding of the risks and environmental impacts of the mining of tar sands. I was also completely unaware that foreign corporations were abusing eminent domain against landowners in my own state and across the country. So I can understand why national leaders were skeptical this far-fetched idea of focusing on a pipeline would actually galvanize the nation let alone get the attention of President Obama.

In today's climate movement, the highlighting of frontline communities, those people most directly affected by fossil fuel activity, has become commonplace, and rightly so. But in 2009, a typical climate change campaign did not work that closely with the people most directly affected by the problem—certainly not with rural farmers and ranchers. Even worse, some environmental groups themselves vilified farmers and ranchers as part of the climate change problem by dismissing biofuels or foolishly saying we could solve everything if we all became vegetarians. Like the cap-and-trade bill, many environmental campaigns were notoriously focused on the D.C. Beltway. Consequently, just like cap and trade, these campaigns lacked the support of farmers and ranchers and even lacked the support of many climate change activists on the ground across America.

After plenty of internal debates and white papers and lots of naysayers, it finally happened. Climate groups ranging from the Sierra Club, the Natural Resources Defense Council (NRDC), the Indigenous Environmental Network (IEN), and later the League of Conservation Voters (LCV), 350.org, and CREDO decided to focus their collective strength on a broad-based national level campaign to oppose the Keystone XL Pipeline. They knew after suffering the cap-and-trade loss that they could not fight the pipeline in D.C. alone. Instead of just arguing about how many molecules of carbon were involved, Kenny and the major environmental groups started reaching out to communities along the KXL proposed route, seeking allies in Montana, South Dakota, Nebraska, Oklahoma, and Texas. This approach, I believe, is what eventually changed the culture in the climate movement. It led to people on the ground and those in policy circles forming a unified campaign. It led to mutual respect and a common fighting spirit formed by doing actions together, by experiencing each other's commitment and unwillingness to back down. Something the Democratic Party also needs to do—work hand in hand with those of us in the states to form a unified campaign.

The campaign's focus on working with frontline leaders is how they found me, a Democrat who had overcome an eating disorder, led the Young Democrats of America, married a cowboy, pushed for health care reform but knew nothing at all about pipelines, tar sands, eminent domain, or climate change. The first call I got from one of these national organizations was from the National Wildlife Federation (NWF), around March 2010, asking if I would attend two upcoming State Department meetings that were billed as government fact-finding sessions for the Keystone XL Pipeline. I was very skeptical. I did not know the environmental landscape either nationally or in Nebraska and could not find a single Democratic elected official in the entire state who seemed to be against the KXL Pipeline project.

At the same time I got the call from NWF, I was receiving phone calls and emails from farmers and ranchers asking if I had heard about a pipeline that would cross over both the largest intact grassland in America, the Nebraska Sandhills, and the Ogallala Aquifer, the main water supply of our agricultural state. Rural people knew my last name from Scott's run for office and from the last few years of my traveling the state nonstop, initially with MTV and Change That Works and now Bold Nebraska. One of those early emails was from Randy Thompson. Randy is a cattleman, and when he walks into a room, you notice him—tall, with a cowboy hat and a confident swagger. He knows just about everyone, since he ran a livestock sale barn for years. He became the face of the Keystone XL Pipeline fight in our early years with our Stand with Randy campaign. Randy described his parents, who worked for years to save enough money to buy the land now being threatened, as "not fancy people, but mighty fine people." Randy was a Republican when the KXL fight started back in 2008. He's now an Independent and uses words like *arrogant* and *son of a bitch* to describe President Trump. Randy wants politicians to care about and work for the people, not for big corporations. And no, Randy is not unique. He is like many rural Americans.

"Hi, Jane, My name is Randy Thompson and I'm from Martell, Nebraska. I am seeking information concerning the proposed pipeline. Our family owns property in Merrick County that will be affected by the proposed Keystone Pipeline. I have been a vocal opponent of the project and have now been threatened with property condemnation if we don't accept the easement proposal offered by TransCanada. I received a certified letter this week giving us thirty days to accept their offer or face immediate condemnation under the power of eminent domain. I find it curious that they can invoke the powers of eminent domain when they don't even have a permit for the project yet. Do you or any of your contacts know if they do indeed have such powers at this time? Any help or advice will be greatly appreciated."

As an organizer first and foremost, I knew I had to at least check out the State Department meetings and see if there was any grassroots energy out there to fight the pipeline. I did this not entirely because of issues related to climate change but because I had come to know farmers and ranchers to be true stewards of the land they love and work every day. Rural people do not often reach out for help, so from the calls and emails I was receiving, like the one from Randy, I already had a sense something was happening. I just had no idea at the time this would be a ten-year journey—more like a roller coaster—that would transform how climate groups operate issue campaigns and how the Democratic Party should organize candidate campaigns.

On May 10, 2010, I attended a State Department meeting in York, Nebraska. Public meetings like this are a requirement in the permitting process for the State Department, which has jurisdiction over pipelines that cross the United States border. A large piece of the pipeline was on display at this meeting, and it literally terrified everyone in the room. Most farmers are used to working with irrigation pipe, which at most is about ten inches in diameter. That piece of the proposed Keystone pipeline had a diameter of thirty-six inches, with the metal thickness of a few dimes. So as people signed in for the meeting, they saw this massive piece of pipe and simply shook their heads. Anyone who did any type of research on the project at all realized this massive pipeline would carry almost one million barrels of tar sands product and other toxic chemicals a day over their land. The very thought of that did not sit well with them at all. Nebraska is an agricultural state, not an oil state. To say that the bureaucrats from D.C. had misread the room is a huge understatement.

Farmer after farmer went to the microphone and told the State Department staff that not only did they oppose the pipeline but they also had deep concerns about the bullying tactics being used by TransCanada to threaten them with eminent domain for the company's own private gain. Susan Dunavan, a short, gray-haired landowner who manages an apple orchard and whose land is covered with prairie grass, stepped up to the microphone and asked, "Why is this pipeline cutting through native grasslands when there is so little such grass left? We have been working over thirty years to establish our prairie. How can you reestablish it?" Other farmers said that TransCanada was blanketing the local media with ads claiming what a good neighbor they would be and yet families are being harassed daily by pushy out-of-state land agents telling them they have to sign now or get no money at all for their land.

The next night a second State Department meeting was held, but this time it was in the heart of the Sandhills at the northern Nebraska town of O'Neill. This is ranch country, and the ranchers there did not speak in polite terms. They were visibly angry; through the entire meeting, many of them had their arms crossed, leaning back in their chairs. They were there to make it clear that this pipeline would never be built. No foreign corporation was going to take their land through eminent domain. While there were a few local environmental leaders present, this was not yet a popular climate change battle, so the room was filled mostly with local ranchers who needed no PowerPoint presentation to tell them how critical land and water was to their livelihoods. One by one the ranchers took the microphone to express their anger about their land and water being threatened by a tar sands pipeline. Only people who do not know the region would be surprised to know that these men and women also went to great lengths to include wildlife in all their discourse. The endangered whooping crane, they said, would be at special risk from any pipeline spills or new transmission lines across the region. In no case was *climate change* the first words out of their mouths. This was a fight about land, water, and their very identity as a people. This was a fight to protect their way of life.

Ranchers stood up to describe the land their ancestors had homesteaded and how it had been passed down from generation to generation. The soil in the Sandhills is fragile and covered thinly with native prairie grass. Not a single pipeline exists in the Sandhills today, and for good reason. The soil cannot be ripped open with massive equipment and then "magically" put back together. Old-timers told of blowouts, incidents in which the thin surface soil erodes away and the wind carves out a hole that the ranchers must quickly cover with hay and old tires before it becomes bigger and bigger. People in the Sandhills have lived there for generations and they know the land well. Clearly, TransCanada officials did not.

Walk into many a house across the Midwestern and Great Plains states, and you'll find prominently displayed a picture of the family's ancestors dressed up in their best clothing, sitting or standing together in front of their barn, dugout, or sod house. Most of their livestock will be with them, and all the furniture in their house will have been dragged out so they can "show off" everything they own. Not many of the subjects in these photos are smiling. Their faces are filled with grit and strength. Not fancy people, but mighty fine people, as Randy would say. Solomon Butcher, a nineteenth-century frontier photographer, documented these settlers planting their family roots in these vast lands. The Homestead Act and later the Kinkaid Act allowed families with little or nothing to claim land on this frontier. The U.S. government gave plots of land from 160 up to, in some areas, 640 acres to families who would commit to making their claim productive. These were policies meant to support working-class families and grow communities outside of the major cities.

This is also a time when our country victimized and took advantage of tribal nations. We brutally forced them off their ancestral lands, making them walk often through blizzards and storms to the barely habitable reservations we were "giving to them." The Native Americans and the buffalo were both decimated in the name of American progress. Old-timers and locals have told me stories of collecting arrowheads along stream banks or tales about their ancestors eating meals with indigenous families. Scott's own great-uncle, Chuck Farritor, told me the story of a young Native American girl teaching him how to catch and train a wild horse. Listening to stories and understanding family roots in rural America are critical to politics in that they enable us to build bridges not only between urban and rural Americans but also between white and indigenous communities. The horrors that our nation put Native Americans through is a tragic history that has never been taken seriously by most Americans, including many in the progressive wing of the Democratic Party. The modern descendants of early Native Americans and the descendants of western homesteaders, even with their troubled common history, are today finding a bond with one another through the love each has for a land that in many ways they both feel is sacred. This is a bond that we found to have powerful political implications in our fight to stop the Keystone XL Pipeline.

On my drive back home from the meeting in O'Neill, I had plenty of "windshield time" to think through the issues brought up at these State Department meetings. Windshield time is literally hours spent looking through the windshield of your car (or minivan or truck) as you drive miles home. It is critical for my work as an organizer. It gives me time to decompress, to reflect on the day's work and on stories I heard, and to plot the next steps. Windshield time also means plenty of time for singing to Lionel Richie, Stevie Nicks, Barenaked Ladies, and listening to plenty of podcasts. If you live in a rural town, you get plenty of windshield time and you collect plenty of road dust. You can't lead or organize from behind a desk.

I had never before taken on the fossil fuel industry, so I was naive about the fight that lay ahead. For me, this was simply a matter of right and wrong. It was about standing up to a big corporation that was telling rural communities they had no power at all and that this pipeline was going to be built whether they liked it or not. I found it shocking that no Democratic officials were in attendance at either of these meetings and that none of them were talking about the injustice of a foreign corporation using eminent domain for its own private gain. Here was the perfect opportunity to stand with rural communities and also to push back against the Republicans, who have traditionally defined themselves as the party of individual property rights. The people in these meetings who had educated themselves on the issues and spoke out forcefully about them were the farmers, the ranchers, their families, local environmentalists, and people of the tribal nations. Although no one knew it at the time, this somewhat strange mix of people would become a powerful unlikely alliance that would turn the climate change movement on its head.

After those first two State Department meetings, I went into organizing mode and never looked back. Even though Bold Nebraska did not start as a group to stop the Keystone XL Pipeline, that issue quickly defined everything we were about to do in the next decade. I began organizing meetings and events along the proposed pipeline route. The sight that greeted me when I walked into those first meetings was lots of cowboy hats and folded arms. Ranchers and farmers were skeptical at first that a Democrat was coming to help protect their property rights and water. Women came around much faster, and with time, honesty, and total commitment, I was able to bring the guys around, too. It's critical to point out that I never hid the fact that I was a Democrat, but I didn't harp on it, either. I made it clear that I believed in climate change and thought the pipeline would make that issue worse. We didn't let our differences tear us apart. We were there together to protect the land and water. We were there to teach each other. I taught them about political strategy and they taught me details about topsoil and every water well that might be particularly subject to pollution. I came to realize they also knew about every species of wildlife on their land and the exact location of all the areas most susceptible to droughts and floods. They seemed to be aware of every blade of grass that might be particularly vulnerable to construction or a toxic spill.

For about a year it was me and a small group of leaders from agricultural entities like the Nebraska Farmers

Union and from organizations like Nebraskans for Peace along with farmers and ranchers holding meetings, rallies, and vigils and conducting various creative actions trying to get the attention of the public as well as state-level politicians. At one point, around Halloween, we carved a message into ninety-one pumpkins to symbolize the ninety-one times a University of Nebraska researcher had said the Keystone XL Pipeline would leak over its lifetime. On another occasion we used a tractor and carved a huge image and message over eighty acres (the same size as eighty football fields) of land. The image depicted the outline of a rancher and an indigenous leader with water lines and the words *Heartland #NoKXL*. This depiction is still the largest piece of political crop art that has ever been done in the United States.

The Republicans should have been falling all over themselves to help protect individual property rights from a foreign corporate land grab. Instead, what we got from them was a chorus of name-calling, accusing us of being "radical leftists," "bottom-feeders," and "job killers." This pipeline, they said, was going to be built, and there was nothing this little group of "fringe lunatics" could do about it. The Republicans were obviously completely out of touch with their own base, and yet the Democrats were also not standing with rural Americans. Some Democratic politicians were concerned about being on the wrong side of those unions who wanted the jobs the pipeline would create. For other Democrats, those elected to office in blue and urban areas, there was just a failure to connect or show concern for the fact that rural America was in the cross hairs of Big Oil.

After about six months of active on-the-ground organizing, I was invited to participate in weekly strategy calls with the national organizations, who at the time crafted their own strategy, mostly focused on messaging around climate change. We strategized endlessly. I learned their world and did my best to explain my own. It was exhausting and often frustrating, but we all learned a great deal about one another and our respective points of view. That was true not only about the pipeline but also about the broader political landscape: How, if we were ever going to truly confront climate change, we needed the voices of rural people to help us shape successful strategies for stopping risky pipelines and fracking projects.

The fossil fuel industry has a track record of targeting rural communities and communities of color, believing them to not have the political will or organizing power to put any of the industry's projects at risk. I mean, when was the last time a massive pipeline threatened a gated community? The playbook used by the pipeline companies is the same one used by coal companies and other big corporations over the years. They come into rural areas or communities of color and tell landowners and residents they cannot stop the project in question. They bribe and bully local elected officials to sign off on permits or grant the company eminent domain rights to complete whatever project they want to build. When I'm told by others that the differences between rural and urban people are just too great to bridge, I ask them to think about the countless American families living in houses they inherited from their forebears that now sit in the shadow of a polluting factory or where the newest sports arena will be built in towns all across the country. How, I ask, is that different from the farmer whose land is being condemned and taken over for a pipeline that's destined to leak countless times?

Although I was initially skeptical, I came to realize that while environmentalists from the national stage may not speak first about the Sandhills, the Ogallala Aquifer, or property rights, as we did in Nebraska, they did care as much as we did about stopping the pipeline. It became obvious to me that we needed one another if we were ever going to stop this reckless project. For my part, I had no idea how to write a white paper on the impact of climate change or to put together a scientific analysis of the contributing effects represented by development of the Canadian tar sands and the Keystone XL Pipeline. What I did know was how to organize people.

It was during the first large-scale action in Washington, D.C., that the "we need one another" lightbulb came on for everyone in the coalition. It was in 2011. President Obama had not yet blocked construction of the Keystone XL Pipeline, even though the climate impacts were documented and the faces of farmers, ranchers, and Native Americans were at the heart of the campaign. President Obama was up for reelection in 2012, and everyone in the #NoKXL movement knew that everything we had done up to this point was on the line. Bill McKibben came up with the idea for this event, and although he did not know me yet, he called to explain his plan. Bill wanted to organize a mass civil disobedience event in Washington, D.C., and he didn't want the event to be populated primarily by white climate activists from college campuses. The people he wanted there were the true frontline voices—the farmers, ranchers, and Native Americans. Bill was asking if I could help him make this happen. Bill, I soon learned, had great respect for all parts of the KXL fight. In his mind, no group was more important than any other. Bill, as well as other green group leaders, truly respected the grassroots groups that had formed and coalesced around this issue. Bill also started 350.org specifically to rock the boat of climate groups, who he thought spent too much time playing the inside game rather than pushing from the outside.

Making the call to landowners and asking them if

they would leave home to get on a plane to D.C. where they would probably be arrested was a big ask. Speaking at a nearby State Department meeting and participating in local rallies was already well outside their comfort zone. Asking them to fly halfway across the country so they could be arrested for civil disobedience was a tall order indeed. Nebraskans, however, answered the call big-time. They flew to D.C. in large numbers and joined a diverse group of other Americans ranging from former Obama staff members to climate scientists like James Hansen, hip-hop organizer Reverend Lennox Yearwood Jr., and numerous leaders of the big green groups. Over a three-day period, over 1,400 people were arrested in one of the largest acts of civil disobedience ever to occur in Washington, D.C.

The White House definitely saw and heard us. What they saw was an unlikely alliance that was so diverse that it demanded attention. The Keep It in the Ground crowd was joined by the Not in My Backyard crowd. And they were united and committed. If the event had included only climate advocates from the coasts and a few national figures, then the White House could likely have simply shrugged it all off. It would take many more creative actions over five years, but finally in November 2015 President Obama rejected the pipeline. Those three days in Washington, D.C., in 2011—in conjunction with our groups putting up twelve tipis on the National Mall for a weeklong encampment and riding horses in the streets of D.C. in 2014—represented a turning point in climate change advocacy. For the first time in the modern period, rural people, both native and non-native, were involved as equal partners in a large political movement. I witnessed the transformation, which was then confirmed when Rohan Patel, a White House senior staff member, left me a voice mail, after years of not knowing if anything we were doing was getting through to the White House, that simply said, "Jane, you have our attention."

I am forever grateful to Kenny Bruno for relentlessly pushing the wacky idea of taking on the expansion of the tar sands pipelines and to Bill McKibben for being the most compassionate leader in the climate change movement. Both leaders knew they needed frontline people involved, and they pushed to make that happen. I took the KXL fight on to help protect the land and water with Nebraska farmers and ranchers and tribal nations. Bill and Kenny never told farmers, ranchers, or moms like me that we were wrong not to see the fight first in a climate change framework. Instead, they treated us with great respect, came to visit our land, taught us a great deal, and also learned just as much from us. Bill and Kenny changed the climate movement more than any other national leaders have been able to do. They did that because they included and embraced an unlikely alliance of people who wanted to pass on to their children the land they love and call home.

Environmental groups needed the faces and voices of rural America to show President Obama and other key decision-makers that the fight to stop the Keystone XL Pipeline was about more than increased carbon emissions. This was about farmers and ranchers. It was about land and water. It was about the sovereign rights of tribal nations. It was about the very heart of our nation, its history and our human ties to the land. Out in the heartland and along the route of the pipeline, we had always known we were not going to win this fight in the halls of Congress. We knew government leaders needed to bone up on their understanding of all the issues involved with tar sands and that they had a lot to learn about us. We also knew it was up to us to educate them, but as for the battle itself, we had always known it would be won in the pastures and cornfields of our own land. As rural people, we could not have won without the national environmental groups and the donors who invested in the small but mighty groups along the proposed pipeline route. And national environmental groups knew they could not win without us.

The unlikely alliance of underdogs winning a major political battle is a key lesson for the Democratic Party. Keystone XL was a David versus Goliath battle. But it was more about everyday heroes who had something to lose and something to prove. Democratic moms, young people, farmers, union workers, and main street business owners all exist in rural towns. We are not unicorns. We want to be heard and taken seriously. We must invest real resources into the red and rural states and build trust with local leaders who know their communities best if we expect to win elections in rural communities. We can and should be learning from each other to change the political landscape in rural America. We can win more seats in the halls of legislatures and Congress if we spend more time in the fields and along the waterways of rural communities across the United States with trust and shared values to build up unlikely alliances. We can find common ground that lifts all families up. In the Keystone XL fight, local groups were engaged and funded. National groups pitched in their skills to lift up rural voices. We all respected one another's role in the collective fight and the shared goal to protect the land and water. There is simply no reason the Democratic Party does not tackle the major political battle of getting Democratic candidates elected in rural America with the same grit and creativity as the pipeline fighters demonstrated. Rural America is filled with working-class heroes who themselves should be running for office and who also yearn for candidates with a backbone to stand up against the status quo. This is who we are as a party, and now we have to show up with the resources and desire to win again with rural people at the table.

THE COWBOY AND INDIAN ALLIANCE

Welcome to the Tribe.

—CHIEF ARVOL LOOKING HORSE

In the fall of 2013, Faith Spotted Eagle, a Yankton Sioux elder and founder of the Brave Heart Society, invited me and the farmers and ranchers I was working with to a treaty signing in rural South Dakota. We were filled with both great excitement and a great deal of anxiety. I had not worked with Native communities and was terrified I might say the wrong thing, or as a group of non-native pipeline fighters, we might not understand the appropriate cultural behavior in a setting as serious as a treaty signing. Faith, over the years, taught me how to be a better ally and how deep trauma and racism are embedded into our daily lives. She did not do that only with her words, although we had many conversations. Faith did this with the actions we both were engaged in to stop the pipeline. I am still learning and working.

As I walked into the room, I was surprised to see cowboy hats, boots, and Wrangler jeans everywhere. I'm not really sure what I expected to see people wearing that day, but it turns out the clothes that are common identifiers of western rural, largely white America are the same as those worn today in rural Native American communities. The room was full of Native American farmers and ranchers. Some farmed, some worked cattle, others buffalo, but in addition to the treaty signing, we were all there for a common purpose: to protect our land and water by stopping the Keystone XL Pipeline.

The day started with both song and prayer, and our Native allies quickly taught us that not all meetings must follow a written agenda. We stood in a circle as a young Rosebud Sioux rancher, Wayne Frederick, who would later get elected as a tribal council member, brought around an abalone shell containing burning sage and sweet grass. After we learned how to smudge properly, we maintained true respect for the process as it unfolded before us.

As we sat together in this room full of fellow pipeline fighters and water protectors, Faith Spotted Eagle asked us to introduce ourselves. One by one the farmers and ranchers from Nebraska told stories of their grandparents learning to farm from the Native Americans who had lived on the land long before their own families arrived. They spoke of times where families, both white and Native American, brought food and shared meals together. Terry Steskal, who goes by Stix, explained through tears how his life has been turned upside down by the threat of the pipeline. Many generations of his family, he said, had lived on and loved the land.

The bitter history of this land was not lost on any of us present at this meeting. I found myself dwelling on the knowledge that all of this great and vast land was first cared for by the native nations, the Lakota, the Dakota, and the Nakota. Most of this land was taken by our government and given to railroad companies and the white immigrants who came in as homesteaders looking for a better life. These homesteaders, the descendants of whom I was now seated with, tragically replaced Native American families whose descendants were also seated among us. And in a great irony of history, here we were, bonding over the one thing we most had in common: a love for and a desire to protect the land and water. It gave the entire setting a surreal sense of history that I'll never forget. In this setting it was impossible not to think about the pain and trauma the United States government put Native American tribes through so many generations ago. And yet in spite of this tragic history, here we were, being treated as honored guests and family. I have never in my life met a group of people filled with such grace and with such a deep, meaningful connection to the land and water as the Native Americans. Our country has for far too long failed to respect them as a people, let alone honor their sovereign and treaty rights.

Everyone in the room took turns telling stories of our families, our backgrounds, the land, the water, and our reasons for fighting the pipeline. One of the elders, Chief Arvol Looking Horse, sat quietly with his head down and arms crossed. He is the Keeper of the Sacred White Buffalo Calf Pipe and speaks about the prophecies of tribal ancestors. He writes often and his words read like commandments to protect the land and water. One written passage said, "We are asking to open your heart and minds to this time of crisis that is now upon us, threatening a healthy life for our future generations and also for the many spirit lives of the four-legged, the winged ones, those that crawl and that swim who depend on Mni Wic'oni, the water of life."

I kept looking at Chief Arvol Looking Horse, and as person after person spoke, he kept his head down and his arms crossed. After the last farmer spoke, the room became very quiet. The chief slowly stood up, opened his arms wide, and said in his deep voice, "Welcome to the tribe."

With those words from Chief Arvol Looking Horse, we all knew we were now on a journey together. We had to protect and stand up for one another. What the government did to Native Nations across our country so many generations ago was now happening to farmers and ranchers today. What the government was doing this time was taking land and giving it to corporations who would use it for their own private gain. For landowners in the path of the pipeline, this was being done through a legal process called eminent domain. Native Americans lost their land through broken promises and broken treaties. In both cases, it was the U.S. government protecting an outside entity over people living on the land. Stories like this are told over and over in western rural communities. Victories are possible, however, and at our meeting, someone spoke of the time when landowners and tribal nations stood together to stop a uranium mine in the Black Hills. That group had united and called themselves the Cowboy and Indian Alliance. At that moment it became clear to all of us that, in our fight to stop the Keystone XL Pipeline, we would carry on the tradition of this name. We would do this, we decided, to honor all the people who had walked this land before us and who had already fought so many battles to protect it. The Cowboy and Indian Alliance would ride once more to protect both the land and Mni Wic'oni.

We all know well the stories of anger, hate, and war that raged between Native Americans and the early white settlers of the American West. Countless movies have been made depicting cowboys and Indians murdering one another. Without question, racism and horrible atrocities occurred as our government actively displaced entire tribes and families. What we don't often hear are the stories of resiliency on both sides, of the shared power arrangements and local unity that often did exist between Native Americans and settlers across many parts of the West. Most Americans are also unaware that this spirit of cooperation is stronger than ever today. Western families, both Native and non-native, are working together to maintain and develop our small rural towns. Native Americans and white landowners are leasing their land to one another for both farming and the raising of livestock. They gather as one at local sale barns, rodeos, and restaurants. Small-town families share meals of fry bread and fried chicken. And now Native Americans and the descendants of white settlers are working together to stop the risky Keystone XL Pipeline.

The lesson is deep for us as Democrats. Healing the distrust our party has left on communities of color and rural towns across our country is necessary and possible. That may seem harsh, but our party has forgotten rural people and especially rural communities of color. We've lost the moral sense of urgency to listen to rural people for solutions to problems. Rebuilding authentic relationships, ones that are not transactional, takes a tremendous amount of time and consumes a lot of resources. We have to truly want rural people engaged in our party and our policy positions, not just to give us their votes. This means our platform and messages will look and sound different, and, I would argue, better. As Democrats, we pride ourselves on a big, inclusive tent. That has to include people we left behind. We have to reach them with humility and a willingness to learn from our past mistakes, knowing those mistakes do not have to define how we build relationships and our party today.

SEEDS OF RESISTANCE

Corn represents many things to the people of rural America. Corn is a huge part not only of the rural economy but of the entire U.S. economy. Farmers raise corn for food, biofuels, coatings for medicine, bioplastics, fiber, and feed for livestock. Corn is also a symbol of our collective resistance to the Keystone XL Pipeline.

We sat in a tipi with strong Nebraska winds blowing outside and a sacred fire burning bright on the inside. Mekasi Camp-Horinek, a member of the Ponca Nation of Oklahoma, was telling us about a dream in which his ancestors visited him with the message he must plant Ponca Sacred Corn in the path of the Keystone XL Pipeline as medicine for the land. In his dream, the elders told him, "When you can no longer stand, the corn will stand for you to protect the land." A small group of farmers and indigenous pipeline fighters had gathered to create the first Spirit Camp on the pipeline route. The gathering was meant to be a space where we prayed and kept a sacred fire. No one expected us all to emerge with such a powerful path forward.

Before the Ponca people were forcibly removed to Oklahoma in the late nineteenth century, eastern Nebraska had been the home of the Ponca Nation. When the government forced them to leave under oppressive heat, swarming insects, storms, famine, and disease, the Ponca families took as much of their corn with them as they could carry. Many families kept the seed in prayer bundles. Because the Ponca Sacred Corn had not touched their ancestral lands of Nebraska in over 130 years, we were not sure we could find enough seed to plant in the pipeline route as medicine. As we sat in the tipi, we talked about Mekasi's dream. We listened to Greg Grey Cloud sing. We ate fry bread and soup. Most of all, together that night, we made plans to bring the Ponca Sacred Corn back to Nebraska.

Mekasi returned to Oklahoma and began gathering seed from the family prayer bundles that still remained among his people. He also discovered seed was being cared for by the Ponca Nation of Oklahoma's agricultural department. In the spring of 2013, Mekasi returned to Nebraska and we were ready. The farm of Art and Helen Tanderup is outside of Neligh, Nebraska; their land lies directly in the path of the proposed Keystone XL Pipeline. Their land is also directly on the path of the Ponca Trail of Tears.

Mekasi drove through the night to be at Art and Helen's farm by sunrise. He walked into the field with a strong heart, offered tobacco, and sang the corn planting song for a good harvest. This sunrise ceremony is personal for Mekasi and the Ponca Nation. It is a tradition handed down through generations.

Handling each kernel of corn with respect and care, we hand-planted eight acres of Ponca Sacred Corn. As we planted each kernel in the soil, we said a prayer for the land. When we planted the first eight acres of corn, we actually had no idea if it would even sprout, let alone grow. For Mekasi, who sang and prayed over every kernel, there was no question it would grow.

For the past six years now, members of the Ponca Nation have returned to their ancestral homeland in Nebraska to plant acres of Ponca Sacred Corn on the Tanderups' farm. The corn has grown every year, and with it, the unity and spirit and strength of the Cowboy and Indian Alliance has grown as well.

Mekasi Camp-Horinek, who also spent time on the front lines of the Dakota Access Pipeline fight, teaches me, pushes me, and is a rural leader Democrats could easily overlook if they did not spend time on the ground. These words from Mekasi root our work:

"Once again we made the journey to the Tanderup farm from Oklahoma to Nebraska on the Ponca Trail of Tears to plant the sacred Ponca seeds of resistance. Not only do we plant in the soil of our ancestors' homeland, we also plant in the hearts and minds of all the people we need to honor and for respect and to protect Mother Earth. It is our hope that the roots of these resistance seeds will spread across the continent and raise the awareness of the fight to stop the Keystone XL Pipeline and protect Mother Earth for all our future generations."

Art and Mekasi decided to take the steps necessary to have the Ponca Sacred Corn seed certified by the U.S. Department of Agriculture. They walked into the local extension office with the seed and an application. The local staff members of the agency did not know quite what to do with Art and Mekasi or their formal request to certify this corn. They both persisted and the local government employees worked hard to make sure the application was treated fairly. Art and Mekasi knew it was critical to get the government to recognize the corn for legal reasons in our pipeline fight. The Ponca Sacred Corn is a cultural resource, and if we could certify it, we would have more grounds to argue the pipeline could not cross this land. Several months later, Art got the letter in the mail. The USDA officially recognized and certified the seed as Ponca Sacred Corn, and there now exists a formal and legal record of the corn's existence.

When those first corn plantings took place, there were no large crowds, no national journalists, and no TV cameras present. At the heart of it all were just two families, one non-native and one native—the Tanderups and Camps—bonded forever by their shared love of the land and water. The Tanderups have a deep respect and empathy for the loss suffered by the Ponca, a loss they now fear themselves. The bond of Native and non-native families is real and goes back decades.

White Buffalo Girl was a young Native girl who died as her family and the entire tribe were forced to walk through Neligh, Nebraska, on the Ponca Trail of Tears. Her mother and father were forced by the U.S. Calvary to keep moving, so they pleaded with local farmers to bury their daughter and honor her life. The farmers and their families agreed to do that and buried the young girl on a grassy hilltop overlooking the Elkhorn River. A few years later the community raised money and placed a marble tombstone on her grave to replace the oak cross they had erected when they buried her in 1877. That marble tombstone still stands today, and every spring, over 140 years later, the people of rural Neligh place flowers and teddy bears on the young girl's grave. Her story and the stories of the Ponca Nation have become part of the local story of Neligh and all the farm families up and down the Elkhorn River valley.

The land has a way of connecting people of many backgrounds. It was in this spirit that the Tanderups made a truly monumental decision. They decided to deed the land on which we had been planting the Ponca Sacred Corn back to its original owners, the Ponca Nations of Nebraska and Oklahoma. This was, for the Tanderups, an act of love for the land, a form of reconciliation, and last but not least, it was also a strong legal strategy. Pipeline companies, like what was happening with the Keystone XL and what had happened at Standing Rock on the Dakota Access Pipeline, will often skirt tribal reservation land so they don't have to formally consult with the tribal governments. By skirting tribal land, the companies can simply hold informal meetings with the tribes, make a few vague promises, and move on with their project. The tribes have no legal ability to stop a project that is not directly on their tribal land. With this move by the Tanderup family, TransCanada now has a legal obligation to engage in formal consultation with the Ponca Nation about crossing tribal land. Negotiations like this were something the company had carefully avoided doing during its entire ten years of trying to complete the KXL project.

On the very day the legal documents were signed deeding the land back to the Ponca Nation, we were harvesting the latest crop of Ponca Sacred Corn. I was walking in the field with Chairman Larry Wright Jr. of the Ponca Tribe of Nebraska, when he turned to me and said, "Every blade of grass on this land carries the DNA of our ancestors." His words stuck with me because the way he sees the land is no different from the way Art and Helen Tanderup view it. The land is everything to them. It carries their ancestors, their legacies, and their entire sense of place.

As our team gathered in the field, Chairman Wright

spoke of the history that we were all now a part of: "This event is another step toward healing old wounds and bringing our people together again on a land that was once ours. When we talk about these issues of eminent domain, the Ponca Tribe is painfully aware of what can happen, how the federal government can make up its mind to erase a nation, to erase a people. Today offers us another opportunity to remember our ancestors who sacrificed the only home they knew. Another opportunity to remember again the relatives and loved ones who died while being removed from their homes. We celebrate this day in their honor and memory, and we must never forget where we came from. We must never forget the sacrifices that have been made by so many among us, sacrifices that have allowed us to be here today. We stand here now with relatives and friends who have shown so much dedication, work, and perseverance in their efforts to protect this land. It is this community of people that will continue to bring us together and continue to protect this precious resource."

Small rural towns, local farmers, ranchers, and tribal nations carried the heaviest loads in the fight to stop the Keystone XL Pipeline. Alongside them are the various national environmental groups as well as donors who ensured we had the resources to put up our strong fight. We also had a strong legal team that never doubted we could win. Dave Domina and Brian Jorde, unlike so many others, never thought of us as "crazy" and never once told us this was a battle we could never win. They effectively used their legal expertise to complement the grassroots actions out in the field. I remember telling Brian about the idea of deeding land back to the Ponca Nation and telling him it would be like creating a "force field" around the Tanderup farm. He did not laugh at me or even blink. He and the Poncas' lawyer Brad Jolly simply went to work. Dave and Brian have been involved in many fights with big corporations. They've witnessed corporate attempts to take advantage of family farms and ranches. Whether the fight involved Tyson's attempt to manipulate the market or the one-sided contracts developed by Monsanto around seed production, Brian and Dave have used their legal skills to help bring balance back into the system.

In our work to stop the pipeline, women are the heart and soul of our work. Helen Tanderup grew up on the land and knows every tree on the home place. After every planting she has also continued to tend the crop throughout the growing season. Women have often been overlooked in some of the great and small battles that have been fought to protect the environment. Casey Camp-Horinek is Mekasi's mother. She's a Ponca tribal council member from Oklahoma and grassroots leader. Her strength is felt immediately, and her words stay with her listeners long after they have been spoken. It was Casey's idea to take the Sacred Ponca Corn to other families across the globe and, through that gift, share with them our grit and resolve to stop risky fossil fuel projects. In her own words, "Ponca Corn has been shared throughout the northern and southern Americas. I have gifted the corn to other indigenous people throughout my travels and have received words of encouragement, gratitude, and prayers for the blessing of the corn. Those who I have gifted it to in South America refer to it as the 'Seed of Resistance.'"

Casey is carrying forward the message of her son's dream, and through the gift of Ponca Corn, all the pipeline fighters and many others as well have become "Seeds of Resistance." We take the words of the elders who came to Mekasi in his dream seriously. We know the corn stands for us when we are not there. We know we must plant seeds of resistance both literally and figuratively if we are going to protect rural communities. The resiliency of farmers and ranchers, their families, and tribal nations cannot easily be put into words. Perhaps that is why a single seed of corn speaks best for us.

To understand why rural Americans stood shoulder to shoulder with environmentalists in fighting this massive fossil fuel project, you need to listen to their stories and understand their deep connection to the land. Everyone in the fight, at the national and local level, put aside areas about which they disagreed in favor of working toward the common and shared goal of protecting our land and water. Without question we sometimes disagreed on strategy or message or the appropriate action to be taken at any particular time, but we were able to work through those conflicts because we built trust in one another. There was no need to have an outside group parachute in for a year to organize people to win this campaign. We had the resources to develop local leaders who organized year-round to win the fight. We always knew that we were the ones that had the most to lose if President Obama approved the pipeline. The national environmental groups, with all their power, understood this and gave us the space to lead the campaign at the local level. The national groups understood all of this and stood back while also making it clear they were there if and when we needed their resources or expertise.

The Democratic Party largely does not do any of this nationwide and certainly does not engage rural communities in a deep and authentic way. Instead, what we see happen over and over again is if a race gets close in a rural district or rural state, they send in outside consultants and staffers to try and win the race. The investments are often too late to close the gap. I am not naive. I understand that there are limited resources in politics and that good, strong Democrats look at the map and look at the lack of voters in rural communities and decide to spend their money in more purple areas. And yet I keep going back to the KXL fight for good reason. No one, not one person, would have looked at that fight on paper and thought a bunch of farmers and ranchers and indigenous leaders would have been the heroes in that story. Every bit of conventional wisdom would have placed investments in D.C. groups to pressure President Obama from the inside. The reason we won is because the national climate groups knew they lost the cap-and-trade fights by only playing the inside, seemingly safe game.

The old Democratic playbook must be thrown out in order to win again in rural communities. We have to believe, because it's true, that there are brilliant people on the ground who understand their state and communities and who can win elections. Just as with the KXL fight, rural states will need partnerships with national groups. The new ideas, new technology, and new ways to reach voters are all things that can be shared with people on the ground. And that sharing needs to go in the other direction, too. Rural leaders in the Democratic Party can explain the policies rural people need trumpeted, issues like market consolidation and eminent domain abuse. We can show the grassroots approach we take to reach voters where they are, including rodeos, sale barns, and churches. We can explain with credibility that some of the online tools like MiniVAN, an app to reach voters with data at the doors, may not work in rural communities because of the lack of cell coverage. Sometimes we just need to be old-school and get back to pen and paper and face-to-face. Or in my case, driving around in my minivan organizing along the way.

The fight against fossil fuel companies with their dangerous pipelines and fracking provides one very useful path for Democrats to reach and reconnect with rural voters. There are other roads as well, including health care, the decimation of family farms because of industrial agriculture, and all the reasons why young people are leaving their rural towns and not coming home. As a party, we have always stood for justice and fairness. We have always stood up for the little guy. Let the Republicans defend corporate America. It's our job to stand up for and with the people.

PART TWO

RURAL PEOPLE AT
THE DEMOCRATIC TABLE

3

WE ALL DO BETTER WHEN
WE ALL DO BETTER

The late great Minnesota senator Paul Wellstone's campaign slogan was "we all do better when we all do better." Wellstone fought for the little guy against big corporations. Wellstone was the perfect example of a Democrat who reached both urban and rural voters. He would often describe why he fought so hard to get elected: "I don't represent the big oil companies, the big pharmaceuticals, or the big insurance industry. They already have great representation in Washington. It's the rest of the people that need representation."

Wellstone raised farmers' concerns about market consolidation among Big Ag corporations while also taking it directly to insurance companies. He worked hand in hand with Senator Hillary Clinton as they worked to pass the Mental Health Parity and Addiction Equity Act. Wellstone listened to a mom from a rural town, Kitty Westin, when she pleaded with him to force insurance companies to cover eating disorders and mental health treatment after her daughter, Anna, committed suicide while battling anorexia. Wellstone was the perfect model of someone who bridged the rural and urban divide. He kept the people, not corporate lobbyists, on speed dial. We need more Democrats like Senator Wellstone. He was from an urban background and yet he showed compassion and empathy toward rural voters. He never sneered at rural people. In fact, Wellstone organized with rural moms on welfare and pushed for policies we still need in place, like all kids receiving free lunch during school. He emphasized rural issues while also making sure urban concerns were tackled in the halls of Congress.

While there are clear differences between urban and rural constituencies, these groups also share some common ground on big issues that rural communities need pushed in state government and in Congress. Policy areas that Democrats can champion to show they stand with rural America are all grounded in the belief that we all do better when we all do better. In fact, the policies that Democrats in big blue states would rate as the most important to them have huge overlap with policies important to rural voters. Climate change. Health care. Corporate overreach. Immigration. Education. We will probably talk about these issues using different words and telling different stories, but we all want major reforms in these areas. None of us want to leave communities behind. We all want a fair shake for our kids.

You often hear broadband being discussed when rural concerns are brought up in political circles and campaigns. We do need access to broadband, and we need it now. There are numerous pockets of America that simply cannot get internet service at all, and cell service is spotty at best. Because our country is increasingly moving online, for everything from banking to paying bills to sharing pictures of grandkids to selling to customers who want more farm-to-table products, rural America needs the government to step in and finally live up to the promises made that broadband access will be expanded. Just as the government did in the 1930s with the Rural Electrification Act, which ensured that rural communities had electricity, and with the Communications Act, which meant that all parts of America could get access to telecommunication, we need to do the same today for broadband. In the 1930s, rural communities did not have access to electricity because the for-profit corporations thought it was too expensive to build out the necessary lines, so they focused on the cities, leaving rural people behind. The government stepped in and made sure there was a level playing field across the United States. My husband's family still has the metal sign that Custer Public Power put up outside their farmstead when they first got electricity: "Robert Kleeb: All Electric Home." That sign went up in the 1950s and made Scott's grandparents tremendously proud. We cannot continue to let for-profit broadband companies be unwilling to provide services to rural communities. With government help, our small-town electric companies could step in to wire our rural towns. We could also be hanging broadband lines as we build new transmission lines across the country to carry the new, clean energy. Rural folks can get this done again just as they did in the 1930s and 1950s. They need allies in the Democratic Party to push legislation to make it happen. Representative Jim Clyburn of South Carolina recently created the Task Force on Rural Broadband, thus focusing a spotlight on this issue. At his famous fish fry, he talked about this issue, describing the plight of students from rural communities, who are often forced to sit in the parking lot at McDonald's in order to get their homework done because their homes and farms have no access to the internet. Clyburn told his local paper: "I'm going to find some creative ways to get this done because there's something wrong with these kids in rural communities being left behind."

As Democrats, we need to prioritize this issue as one of the first steps in bridging the urban and rural divide. Even though access to broadband is critical, we also cannot let it be the beginning and the end of a rural policy platform. I am an organizer in my heart and in my work, so as I take you through policy areas that urban and rural Democrats can stand with each other on, understand that these are just *some* of the areas where we can start to reconnect with rural voters.

BIG IDEAS TO STAND WITH RURAL AMERICA

- **Health Care for We the People:** Rural hospitals are closing at an alarming rate. There are huge scarcities of mental health care practitioners and specialists to help people recover from illnesses. Expanding Medicare and Medicaid are top priorities, along with building on successful programs to train and keep health professionals in rural towns.

- **End Eminent Domain for Private Gain:** Ending eminent domain abuse and focusing on land justice works hand in hand with the need to stop the build-out of new fossil fuel infrastructure and massive industrial ag projects that accelerate climate change.

- **Confront Climate Change:** Rural communities rely on the land for their livelihoods. They are on the front lines of climate change. They need to be at the table providing solutions because they already are confronting climate change with biofuels and regenerative agricultural practices.

- **Level the Ag Playing Field:** Industrial and corporate agriculture is squeezing out family farmers, who live on razor-thin margins. Deals are cut on the state and federal level to protect Big Ag. We must get back to supporting families and local food systems.

HEALTH CARE FOR WE THE PEOPLE

Many farmers and their spouses work off the farm
for health insurance. We need regulations that put
people before profits.

—JIM KNOPIK, FAMILY FARMER

As a teenager, I struggled with a deadly eating disorder that required professional long-term treatment. One day I was sitting in a room where many of us would go to write between treatment and therapy sessions, and a woman walked in, tears streaming down her face. It turned out she had gained one pound and her insurance company decided she no longer fit into their "eating disorder guidelines." They would, as a result, no longer pay for her treatment. She had been there only a short time and was not ready to leave. She needed comprehensive mental health treatment, but her insurance company was more interested in saving money than it was in saving her life.

I saw this story repeated over and over again. Families having to mortgage their homes or, even worse, turn their children over to the government as wards of the state so they could get treatment under Medicaid. I was lucky that even though my own middle-class family could never have paid for the long-term treatments I needed, my grandmother could. She was a trailblazer who had started one of the first Burger King restaurants in Florida, a feat that for a woman in those days was almost unheard of. My grandmother used her savings to keep me alive.

Recovering from a mental illness changes one forever in countless ways, but the change I want to emphasize here is the political awareness the process brought to me. I saw firsthand the injustice of big corporations and saw our government not stepping up to force the insurance company to do the right thing and to honor its commitment to protect its citizens. The day I watched that woman leave the treatment facility, I promised myself I was going to do everything I could to fight injustice and show up for people trying to force the change that was needed.

My experience recovering from an eating disorder drives everything I do in politics today and explains why I take on what others might say are hopeless fights. These fights have included taking on Big Oil, battling racial injustice in the public schools, working to address the failure of the Democratic Party to invest in the youth vote, and now making the case to Democrats that we must bridge the rural and urban divide. I'm proud of the grassroots campaigns I've had the honor of working on over the past twenty years. I do this work because I feel an obligation to my grandmother, my family, and those who work hard trying to live a good life but find themselves fighting forces who seem to be telling them that their way of life and even their very existence is dispensable.

Mental health care is essentially nonexistent in rural America. Families have to wait six months to get an appointment or drive for hours to see a medical professional. Many of us live in rural America because we cherish the wide-open spaces and the low population density, and yet the vast distances between places can be isolating. Most politicians have no idea just how long it can take to get to lifesaving treatment. The stigma attached to mental illness still keeps people from getting the care they need, which makes getting better even more difficult. Suicide rates are higher in rural America than in urban communities. Rural America now faces a full-blown health care crisis, what with the lack of mental health care and the dearth of specialists to help people recover from illnesses.

In "Who's Going to Take Care of These People?" a recent article in *The Washington Post* about the number of rural hospitals closing, Eli Saslow tells the story of one in Fairfax, Oklahoma. The hospital is the only place for care within thirty miles. Staff were donating their time to keep the hospital open, knowing people would die otherwise. For all the recent talk about protecting rural communities, no one is coming in to save this hospital or the other hundred in rural towns that have closed their doors recently. Rural hospitals see all the health issues inner-city hospitals see, from obesity to addiction to diabetes. As Republicans slash Medicare and Medicaid budgets at the federal and state level, rural hospitals suffer the most because the towns are older and have more poverty than most urban communities. The fact that rural communities have a larger population of older Americans makes sense to most people. We've all heard the stories of "brain drain," leaving rural towns with mostly older residents. But the level of poverty in rural towns is often overlooked and simply not discussed. This is a double whammy for rural hospitals, resulting in closed doors.

When we were organizing for SEIU during the fight for Obamacare, we did not encounter the same protests and anger about passing health care reform in the rural towns as we did in the larger cities of Lincoln and Omaha. In the rural towns, people came to the grass-roots meetings and the town halls Senator Ben Nelson was hosting to tell stories of how their hospital was about to close, which meant jobs and lifesaving care would go away. Jim Knopik, a family farmer who is now building solar installations on farms and ranches across Nebraska, sees the changes in his community because of the rising costs of insurance. Not only are more families taking second jobs in town so they can get access to health insurance, but families are simply moving away. "There were once 49 families within two miles of our farm, there are now only five," he told the *Grand Island Independent* during 2009 when we were fighting for Obamacare. "The remaining family farmers and main street businesses, the economic engines of our community, are struggling. Many farmers and their spouses work off the farm for health insurance. This often prevents farm families from growing their farming operations and developing profitable new enterprises."

I saw an ugly side of politics up close and very personal during those years of organizing for health care. The yelling and massive rallies against the government's role in health care happened in the big cities, not in the small towns, and it was a stark contrast. I still remember showing up at a Republican rally to stop health care reform in Omaha and seeing a guy dressed up in a clown outfit carrying a sign reading "Hello Ration Care, Goodbye Grandma" or another sign carried by an older woman: "No socialized medical care. Yes fix Medicare," which is of course an unbelievable juxtaposition of ironic opposites. Others carried all sorts of racist signs about how "illegal aliens" were going to take health care away from citizens. There were guys wearing T-shirts with images of guns and "peace through superior firepower" scrawled on them.

All I could think about as I walked through the angry crowd in Omaha were the positive events I had witnessed in rural communities that were not being captured by the media. For example, at ones of the small towns we held a meeting in, an older farmer came and sat at the same table as an African American small-business owner. The farmer started to tell us how he has health care now because of Medicare, but he was worried about his kids and grandkids not being able to farm because they cannot afford the costs of insurance on the market. The small-business owner, who happened to own a car washing service that all the farmers knew, since he worked magic on their very dirty pickup trucks, mentioned similar concerns. He was terrified he would fall between making too much for Medicaid for his kids but not enough to buy insurance on the private market. I heard these stories in small town after small town. Black, white, Latino, and Native American families were all living with the same fears, and yet as Democrats we somehow let the Tea Party trump the narrative told about the real need for health care reform. We lost a true public option because we did not push back using stories from rural communities across the country. Democrats never confronted the Republicans representing these rural areas because for political operatives these towns are written off as not winnable. Democrats did not even think about going to a rural town to showcase such a story. Rural families were simply ignored by national Democrats during the fight to pass Obamacare.

Expanding Medicare and Medicaid are top priorities for rural areas, along with building on successful programs to train and keep health professionals in rural towns—dentists included, who are always overlooked when the conversation is about health care professionals. In small towns, the doctors often all come together to offer a free day of dental care, and you see everything from chipped teeth to cavities and infections so bad patients need to be admitted into the hospital. These days of free care are inspiring and yet heartbreaking, because you also see moms and dads waiting all day hoping their kid will be one of the lucky ones to get in before the dentists have to close for the day and the sadness in parents' eyes when you see them pack up their folding chairs when they realize their children will not get their chance this year.

Farmers and their spouses often take a job in town so they can get access to health insurance. Family farmers and ranchers are small-business owners and must self-insure, which means the costs are unsustainable for families already living on razor-thin margins. This is true not just for farmers but for many people living in small towns, who are all mostly working in small businesses they started or their friend started. The options for buying health care insurance on the market are shrinking and the deductibles are rising.

Whenever I talk to doctors, dentists, and nurses in

small towns, they always bring up the need to expand Medicare and Medicaid since that is what keeps their doors open. They complain all the time about the endless paper work required by insurance companies and the constant changing of policies. Small doctors' offices often have to hire staff members just to process paper work for the insurance companies. Just as is true with climate change, I maintain we need rural voices at the table for solutions. Our small town doctors and nurses are also fully capable of coming up with great ideas about improving our rural health care—like a Nebraska program involving small rural universities and colleges, where they give a full scholarship to young people from rural towns who commit to working in rural towns after they graduate. Entire books are written on the crisis we have in our country's health system. For rural America, it is all compounded because our hospitals are closing and many professionals are moving to find work. In the meantime, voters are taking matters into our own hands.

Red and rural states including Nebraska, Idaho, and Utah all passed expanding Medicaid by a vote of the people in the 2018 election cycle. The vote by the people means over 300,000 more Americans will receive access to the care they need in these states. Even though the measures passed overwhelmingly in these states, the Republican governors are not making it easy to implement the policies, showing even further how one-party rule in many states hurts families. Republicans, like those in Nebraska, are focusing on the price tag, which will be about $150 million. Those same Republicans never focus on the money that will now come into our state, roughly $1.4 billion in federal funds we now qualify for with the passing of the law. You can look at these votes and shake your head, feeling frustrated that voters are passing ballot campaigns like expanding Medicaid and increasing the minimum wage and yet vote for candidates who are against these critical issues. Or, we can start to connect the issues with the candidates' campaigns and start getting wins in both areas.

The Democratic brand is damaged with rural voters, and we have work to do to build trust again in small towns around the country. Voters are with us on values and issues—for example, in 2014, 60 percent of Nebraskans voted through a ballot initiative to increase the minimum wage—but Nebraska has not elected a statewide Democrat since 2006. Something not often talked about is the fact that the ballot campaigns, like expanding Medicaid and the minimum wage, have the financial resources needed to win. Outside groups and unions provide the money and hire strong local campaign staff to win these efforts on the ballot. No one really wants to talk about this huge gap in funding for Democratic politics. We are winning *issue* campaigns in red states but not *candidate* campaigns. It is not because people hate

Democrats and love the issues we advocate for. No, it is much simpler. Winning statewide is possible in red and rural states as a Democratic candidate *if* you have the money to win. If the same amount of funds needed to win Medicaid expansion—roughly $2 million—would be invested in statewide candidates, along with the needed strong state party infrastructure, you would see massive gains in the Democratic column. We can start to turn the tables around for rural health care if we go beyond funding ballot campaigns and start funding the state parties and candidates in red and rural states.

END EMINENT DOMAIN FOR PRIVATE GAIN

Nobody wants to be told someone's going to come in and take your land, and it doesn't matter what political bent you are.

—JULIA TRIGG CRAWFORD, TEXAS FARMER

During the height of building railroads and interstate highways, the government used a policy called eminent domain to seize land in order to build massive public projects. Eminent domain was supposed to be restricted for "public use" projects, essentially infrastructure that the public can use and benefit from all across the country. Today, eminent domain is being used for private gain from projects like huge sports arenas to massive export pipelines. I understand some Democrats think eminent domain is needed to build out clean energy or to reclaim land polluted by Big Oil. I admit this is an issue I am deeply passionate about and have a really bright line on. I do not think any private gain project should use eminent domain—even for clean energy.

Tom and Cathie Genung are some of the most dedicated pipeline fighters. They give endless amounts of time to prepare food for meetings, create seed bundles of the Ponca Sacred Corn, and help travel to farmers' and ranchers' houses to talk one-on-one about TransCanada's latest threats. One day back in early 2008, Cathie's mom got a knock at the door. She was in her late seventies, a widow, living on the family's ranch in the Sandhills. Trans-Canada informed her they would use eminent domain to seize her land if she did not accept the offer they gave her. No discussing the project, no listening to where a better place might be for the pipeline on their home place, and no waiting to see what the environmental review said about the risks of the project. Either you sign your land away for pennies—since the easement contract is forever, but they pay you only once—or we'll go to court. Worse, they lied to her, saying if she did not sign she would not get any money and they take the land anyway. This type of threat is issued every single day by land agents that Big Oil pipeline corporations send out to rural communities. They prey on older landowners, rural people, and communities of color. They think these folks have no political power and it is easy to run roughshod over them.

The Republican Party used to be the political center for property rights. When the *Kelo v. City of New London* decision came down from the U.S. Supreme Court, a case that paved the way for corporations to take advantage of governments' right to authorize the use of eminent domain, you saw Republicans pretending their hair was on fire and introducing state bills that supposedly restricted the use of eminent domain. It was all a sham. What really happened was Republicans did in fact introduce and pass eminent domain laws, but they gave huge carve-outs to pipelines and other risky fossil fuel projects. They also gave carve-outs for other private gain projects. Republicans in essence lied to voters, running and winning campaigns to get elected to state legislatures across the country using property rights as a major platform of their candidacy and of course leaving out the fine print that pipelines and other private gain projects could still use eminent domain to advance their interests.

Today, members of the Republican Party are total hypocrites when it comes to eminent domain and local control. On one hand, you have President Trump saying on stages across the country: "I love eminent domain, it's how I build my hotels." And then on the other hand, in legislatures across the country, Republicans are using the shell game once again, passing laws that say clean-energy projects like wind farms cannot use eminent domain. They then go out into the community and get headlines written in the local papers that say once again Republicans are the party of property rights. The only thing is, wind farms and other clean-energy projects do not have eminent domain rights in the first place. So these bills are meaningless when it comes to the law. Republicans cleverly use these new laws to further wedge urban and rural voters apart and to lie to voters, maintaining that they are protecting property rights when all they are doing is demonizing clean energy. I am a property rights advocate who strongly believes eminent domain for private gain must end everywhere. A corporation should not be able to knock on your door and say they are taking your land for a project they will make a bunch of money on. Democrats are nowhere to be found on this issue, and it is one that resonates not only in rural America but urban America, too.

No corporation should be allowed to use eminent domain for private gain. No governmental agency, local, state, or federal, should be able to use eminent domain for "public use" and then turn around and give that land to a corporation for its private gain. Yet this is happening all over our country in rural and urban communities. In cities, eminent domain abuse happens when homes that have been in the hands of families get torn down to make room for yet another football stadium. In rural towns, land is being handed over to Big Ag and pipelines so they can line the pockets of their shareholders. We need to end eminent domain for private gain, something we can accomplish only if urban and rural leaders come together at the state and national level to pass the laws needed to protect the land, the water, and our homes.

Sometimes I hear people pushing back on ending eminent domain for private gain because, they say, "you cannot have a single person holding up a project." When it comes to building a highway that will connect towns and cities for public use, this is a valid point. When it comes to building a massive pipeline that will damage land and water and increase climate change impacts, it is rarely one person holding up a project. It is often hundreds who get bullied and harassed by big corporations using deceptive practices to grab their land.

Too often rural communities are written off as powerless, which is often why big corporations come into our towns and run roughshod over our land and water. This is true for white rural communities and rural communities of color. We know our water is all connected. We know tribal ancestors worked and walked this land long before the rest of us. For decades, both the sovereign rights of tribal nations and the property rights of farmers and ranchers have been trampled on by fossil fuel corporations.

I traveled down to Paris, Texas, not for the great barbecue (although they definitely have it), but because I wanted to stand with Julia Trigg Crawford, a family farmer and rancher who was battling TransCanada in court, in an oil state, to try and save her family's land from eminent domain abuse. Nothing about her strength, grit, or determination surprised me. She is a fighter who shouldered much of the stress of her fellow landowners during these years of court battles. What did surprise me was not a single Democratic leader was there from Texas standing with her.

One way to get land justice for families facing big corporations attempting to take their land is to end eminent domain for private gain. We must also strengthen the consultation process for tribal nations so they have final say on projects that get built on their sovereign land. Rural people's entire stories and livelihoods are tied to the land. If there is one policy the Democratic Party can take up that is unexpected and will result in more rural people taking notice while also furthering the values we hold as a party, it is to end eminent domain for private gain.

CONFRONTING CLIMATE CHANGE AND THE FIGHT ON THE HORIZON

Our land is everything.

—REPRESENTATIVE DEBRA HAALAND

In order to confront climate change, we need to stop building new fossil fuel projects that lock us into more carbon pollution for another sixty to a hundred years, the life-span of these projects. In many places, the previous sentence is controversial yet pretty obvious, and you do not need a science degree to come to this conclusion. Instead, we need to grow more biofuels and build a whole fleet of clean-energy projects to power America. In order to build the massive amounts of clean energy and transmission lines needed to carry this new energy, we need lots of land. Guess where the land is? Primarily in rural America. Guess where most climate change education and outreach are happening? Not in rural America. We saw with the KXL Pipeline, fracking, and many other fights across the country that rural people step up in big ways to push back on fossil fuel corporations who want to take the land and pollute the water. But—and there is a big but here—when it comes to involving rural people in the plans to confront climate change, especially in regard to plans to build out massive clean-energy projects, they are ignored, forgotten, and worse often blamed as part of the problem. It does not have to be this way.

When I heard Representative Deb Haaland of New Mexico, who along with Sharice Davids of Kansas were the first Native American women elected to Congress, say to a crowd of Democratic donors, "Our land is everything," I knew we were at a moment where we might just be able to break through the traditional lens of climate change and energy policy. Representative Haaland is transforming the way our party looks at how fossil fuels impact the land and the people. She is breaking through old barriers that would often stifle strong ideas. We are in a moment and she is the voice many of us have been waiting for in order to make it clear we need to protect the land and water. Both Native and non-native families often come together and stand together despite our differences and different backgrounds when it comes to the land and water. We know that if only some of our communities are protected in legislation, then none of our communities are protected. We need one another to confront climate change, and we need to listen to those who live and work the land in ways we simply have not done before.

I was recently in a room with environmentalists, union leaders, utility directors, and Democratic Party officials to start the discussion on how we could avoid the pitfalls we have seen in blue states where they get right up to the finish line in passing a big clean-energy bill only to see it go down in flames because unions rightfully get concerned about the good-paying jobs their members have in the fossil fuel industries that will disappear. It was our first meeting, and a predictable moment of tension came up when I reminded everyone that we might not agree on projects facing our state like the Keystone XL Pipeline, but we do agree that clean energy is essential—to confront climate change, to create jobs, to keep young people here, and to attract new tech companies moving into Nebraska. We were discussing wind farms, transmission lines, and setbacks (the distance between turbines). The union guys started to get defensive; one of them said, basically, that we rural folks wanted it both ways. We wanted all this clean energy without pipelines, but the energy has to be moved via transmission lines that would run through the Sandhills, where the wind comes from, but we were against that, too. I hear this a lot, so I explained that rural people have ideas on how they want these clean-energy projects to be built. They want to see some of the clean energy they are helping generate stay in their own town. They want to see the benefits of energy generation lower their electric bills. They want a say as to where the best places would be for the turbines and transmission lines, and since they have lived in the community for generations, they often know better how to avoid the wet meadows, fragile soil, and migrating birds.

Rural families and small businesses also have a massive problem that new transmission lines can help solve. Rural communities badly need access to broadband. Rural hospitals, small businesses, farms, and schools are all hurting because of the lack of this access. Wind companies and utilities could come into a town and offer to install broadband lines on the transmission projects. Wind companies already offer fair, for the most part, land contracts for the turbines to be placed on someone's farm and ranch. Wind companies also generally have solid decommissioning plans for when a turbine is past its life-span to ensure money is set aside to take down the structure and restore the land, unlike pipeline companies, who leave their rotting pipeline in the ground. I explained all of this in one breathless monologue. When I finished, I asked, "So, what do you think? Is all of that doable?" The union guys all smiled and said, "Yes, if you remember to add in good-paying jobs with training and benefits that can support a family."

It is not enough to talk about a "just transition," which is what I often hear when I am in D.C. or on the coasts. Union workers hear "just transition" as code to mean your job is not needed anymore, so you will be given a job that pays half your original salary, which means your dignity is also halved. We need to build an entire new energy infrastructure to actually confront climate change. Workers who will construct the projects and people who live on the land need to be involved in the planning from the beginning, not added on as second thoughts or seen as window dressing in a community presentation.

Just like we need to get our relationships right with unions, we also need to get our relationships right with rural America. At this point, rural communities don't really trust the Democratic Party. Misinformation and conspiracy theories abound, like President Trump proclaiming wind turbines cause cancer. Look, Big Oil has been around this block before and they see the handwriting on the wall. So, taking a page out of the Republican handbook, they see clean energy as a wedge issue between rural and urban, between Republicans and Democrats. And it is working. You are seeing rural communities zone out wind. You are seeing states end the use of clean energy on new transmission lines. None of this is good news.

For the last several years, resistance to the build-out of clean energy is bubbling up at zoning boards in rural towns and state legislatures across the country, especially in the so-called red states. Some of the opposition is based on local concerns, but some of it is derived from fossil fuel corporations and groups like the American Legislative Exchange Council (ALEC) who write model bills for conservative Republicans to push. The bills and zoning regulations are all focused on wind and solar energy. Specifically, corporations and conservative groups want to protect their own interests but also stymie truly effective wind and solar solutions. For example, you are seeing laws that are sold as protecting property rights when in fact they are laws to zone out wind. The best way to tell if Republicans are really standing up for property rights is to add language to their new bills that make it clear the regulations will also apply to pipelines, oil wells, and fracking. Watch them drop the proposed legislation like a hot potato.

JUST AS RURAL COMMUNITIES CAN BE SEEN AS PART OF THE SOLUTION ON clean energy and climate change, we can also be part of the solution when it comes to agriculture and climate change. One of the biggest areas is growing more biofuels. Nebraska Corn Growers and other major Ag groups started to push back on President Trump as he gave refinery waivers to Big Oil corporations including Exxon Mobil. We need more biofuels on the market to combat climate change and to spur rural economies. What Trump is doing means we are shutting off the ability to blend biofuels at refineries, which only adds insult to injury to family farmers. More Democrats and climate groups needs to stand with farmers as they push back and fight for cleaner fuels.

Nebraska congressional members hold a breakfast once a week in Washington, D.C., to give visitors a chance to ask questions and hear updates from their representatives. I was in D.C. for a Democratic National Committee meeting and in attendance at this breakfast when news reports came out about the Green New Deal. The headlines were not good for rural America. Jokes were flying around the city about banning hamburgers and farting cows. At the breakfast I felt compelled to stand up and apologize. Yes, apologize for the way Democrats had rolled out this policy. I stood there and turned to a room of Nebraskans and said, "First, let me apologize for any Democrat that's been out there saying that we should not be eating meat or drinking milk. The Nebraska Democratic Party fully supports farmers and ranchers and knows that they're already confronting climate change."

I was not the only one pushing back on the rhetoric and unfortunate draft version of talking points that was leaked online from Congresswoman Alexandria Ocasio-Cortez's office. In fact, the young people of the Sunrise Movement were some of the first people to reach out to me, asking how they can work with rural communities and family farmers. Young people understand there is a difference between massive corporate agriculture and families who do everything they can to protect the very land that their livelihoods are tied to. There is nothing in the Green New Deal about banning cows, but it is a stereotype of urban Democrats that sticks. A young Kansas rancher, Brandi Buzzard Frobose, went online and wrote a great letter telling her story: "As a rancher, I am proud to produce safe, healthy and affordable beef for a hungry nation. We are producing beef in the United States more sustainably and efficiently than ever before." She went on to say: "The U.S. produces nearly 20% of the world's beef with only 9% of the world's cattle. That's pretty amazing and tells a great story of our efficiency using the resources available to us!"

Our hasty generalizations about agriculture are, more often than not, based on misinformation and outright ignorance. It's easy to do. In fact I am sure if you live in a city, you could cite examples of rural people stereotyping where you live. This is a two-way street, no doubt. You might be surprised to know most of rural America is opposed to industrial agriculture. Rural Americans want to see climate change confronted because they know their livelihoods rely on action being taken now. Farmers and ranchers are, in many ways, the first and best environmentalists. I heard Cory Booker—the United States senator from New Jersey and a former mayor of Newark—describe farmers as the first entrepreneurs. He is 100 percent accurate. Rural people see problems and figure out solutions. They do not wait around for anyone to save them. They fiercely protect the land and water. They might not call themselves environmentalists; instead, they often say they are stewards of the land or talk about conservation. They also might not use the words *climate change,* but even that has changed in the last few years. Climate change is the biggest issue our nation faces, and people who live in rural America have the very land our country needs to confront this massive issue. And yet they are rarely if ever consulted as policies and messaging documents, like the Green New Deal talking points, get drafted. This is a major oversight of the Democratic Party and we need to fix it.

I both support the Green New Deal—which, it should be noted, is not a bill but a resolution, a suggested framework for future legislation—and still speak very loud and clear on how farmers, ranchers, and rural communities must be included in that solution. As Democrats and progressives work on the Green New Deal and any other climate bills, it is critical we don't ignore rural voices. That sense of unity will be difficult when the Democratic Party does not have enough rural members elected at the state and federal level. If you don't have people in the room who have lived or worked on family farms and ranches, then stereotypes or misunderstandings easily lead to one-sided policies.

I've been talking about the Green New Deal as if it's a policy that has been on the table for decades. So let me provide some background on this creative approach to confronting climate change. The Green New Deal is a proposal for a massive investment, of the magnitude of Franklin Delano Roosevelt's New Deal of the 1930s, to move the U.S. economy from fossil fuels to clean energy while creating millions of good jobs. Concepts like this have been presented before, yet we are still at a point where our national and state governments do not take climate change seriously and do not have key stakeholders at the table. I appreciate that Representative Ocasio-Cortez and Senators Edward Markey of Massachusetts and Jeff Merkley of Oregon are challenging the status quo and bringing attention to the critical issue of climate change.

When I saw the early drafts of the Green New Deal, I reached out to the young people leading the Sunrise Movement and mentioned that the only reference to rural concerns or agriculture was a single line stating the agriculture industry needed to reduce their emissions. If you do not know about the Sunrise Movement, look them up—the young people are truly leading the way and pushing leaders to take climate change seriously. Plenty of people in agriculture already know this and are already working hard to make operations more efficient and to do everything to protect the health of the soil and water. Backs will get up real quick if urban members do not recognize this reality and see rural constituents as a problem and not part of the solution.

FDR's New Deal, while admirable in many ways, shortchanged African Americans, Latinos, and women by largely exempting domestic and agricultural workers from newly enacted programs such as minimum wage laws and Social Security. Programs designed to build housing for those who desperately needed it were largely unavailable to African Americans and Latinos. Similar mistakes must not be made again now in the Green New

Deal, which has clearly taken into account traditional frontline communities of color and still has a long way to go to fully include rural families.

We also have to acknowledge that without the establishment of massive public works programs to build and maintain useful infrastructure, our union brothers and sisters can be hurt by the termination of new fossil fuel projects. We must protect the dignity of their livelihoods and commit to protecting their rights while providing a real, comparable salary for their hard work. Unions built our country and we will not leave them behind. New jobs in the solar and wind industries sound good, but they are largely not union jobs. Workers in the coal mines making $50 an hour are not going to be able to sustain their families with jobs installing solar for $20 an hour. Our country must face the fact that we have affordable energy because for decades the fossil fuel industry has been propped up by massive subsidies. Unquestionably fossil fuels facilitated the growth and development of our country. But these subsidies must end and be shifted toward clean energy so workers can sustain their families while building out the energy sources that help us solve climate change.

I'M NOT A POLICYMAKER, BUT I DO HAVE A UNIQUE PERSPECTIVE BASED ON MY involvement in the fight against the KXL Pipeline, my work as an organizer, and my personal life as a neighbor in rural America who listens to what folks are saying. Maybe it would be easier if we could just close a coal plant and build more wind and solar to power our communities and that would be the end of that story. There are people and families and land involved, so it is not that easy. Our country has allowed big corporations to control the types of energy favored, where the energy is generated, and who it is sold to. We've been told we do not get a say in the process because when we flip a light switch on to power our homes, energy is there and it is reliable. This system worked for us for decades, but now the entire equation has to be flipped because we know the devastation climate change brings to our communities with continued fossil fuel development. In a 2016 exchange with coal workers, Senator Bernie Sanders nailed the response to climate change. He made it clear he believed in climate change and acknowledged that jobs in the coal industry had been declining since the seventies. He then looked at a young coal miner and said: "I do not hold this gentleman and the coal workers responsible for climate change. In fact I think these guys are heroes. I grew up in a rent-controlled apartment, and I will never forget the piles of coal that kept my house warm." Sanders then went on to say our nation must make good on the pensions the coal miners earned; he also stressed the need to reinvest money into communities devastated by climate change. We can acknowledge the hard work, not leave anyone behind, and make it clear where we stand on the changes we must make now.

Unlikely alliances between tribal nations, farmers, ranchers, and environmentalists, like the ones that developed during the KXL Pipeline campaign, can be a model for how to shape legislation to address climate change. Rural communities have a profound bond with the land and water and take actions every day to address climate change, from water sensors to cover crops, from increasing buffalo herds to improving the soil, from growing biofuels to building wind and solar to bring power to our homes, farms, and ranches. Energy and climate change are at the very heart of how our country will move forward. Our kids and grandkids are literally depending on us to get this right. If we put people at the center, we can create a fair energy system that is not killing the planet. Or we can allow big corporations to continue lining the pockets of politicians who have a spine when campaigning but forget who sent them to create systematic change once in office. Democrats can and should be leading on confronting climate change by creating an entire new energy infrastructure. The only way we can do this is to bring rural people and tribal nations to the table. They have the land. We need to respect this, or we will just keep on spinning our wheels with white papers and fancy words like *just transition* when we could be putting power back in the hands of the people.

RURAL SOLUTIONS TO CONFRONT CLIMATE CHANGE

Rural communities are confronting climate change and need to be seen as full partners in developing any climate policy. Renewable energy now makes up 17 percent of our country's energy sources. Most of the wind energy is being built in rural communities. If we care about climate change, we need to care about our rural neighbors. Rural voices and ideas will make climate policies stronger. Here are just a few things rural communities, family farmers, and ranchers are doing now to confront climate change and get back to regenerative agricultural practices:

- Using water sensors to reduce usage and protect aquifers.

- Planting cover crops to reduce soil erosion and serve as a carbon sink.

- No-till farming, which means leaving the stubble from last year's crops in the ground, saving time and fuel and providing a carbon sink.

- Growing biofuels, from corn to switch grass, that produces less greenhouse gas emissions than traditional fossil fuels.

- Feeding the stock from biofuels to cattle and hogs as a high-energy by-product instead of adding it to landfills.

- Turning manure into energy.

- Rotational grazing to protect grasses and add to the biodiversity of plants. This also prevents overgrazing and creates a better ecosystem, including more organic matter in the soil and increased drought resistance.

- Installing clean energy from windmills to solar.

- Expand hemp production to (among other things) replace oil-based plastics and absorb CO_2.

LEVEL THE AG PLAYING FIELD

One of the easiest areas for Democrats to find common ground is opposition to corporate encroachment in rural communities. In meetings I held all over Nebraska, this issue comes up over and over again. Once I went to supper at the house of a farmer who had started a group to stop Costco from coming into their small town of Nickerson. Costco was trying to build a massive number of chicken barns to feed the $5 roaster addiction that has swept suburban America. In order to process up to a million chickens a day, Costco needs lots of farmers buying into their one-sided contracts that keep farmers in a cycle of debt and risk our soil and water.

The farmer's table was overflowing with homegrown food. (A major side benefit of working alongside farmers and ranchers is you always leave with homemade bread, fresh eggs, or some really good meat.) Over this supper of fresh tomatoes, potato salad, and locally raised chicken, we were discussing property rights and clean water. Another topic of our conversation was the fight to end vertical integration of agriculture. Vertical integration is a major problem in rural communities. A big corporation like Tyson will come in and promise farmers and ranchers a ten-year contract to buy their product. On the face of it, such a promise sounds awesome in the unpredictable world of ag. But there is a catch. The only place the farmer or rancher can sell their product to is Tyson (or Costco or Hormel or some other industrial food company). So that immediately cuts out competition and getting the best price possible for your product. On top of this, the farmer also needs to meet very strict specifications as to how to raise the chicken or hog. This usually includes building a barn of sorts with specific dimensions and using feed only from that corporation, as well as a long list of other demands. All of this results in farmers taking out loans. Once the loan for the barn is paid off, some ten years later, the company comes out with updated specs the farmer now has to adhere to, leaving farmers in a constant cycle of debt.

So on this topic I am on very solid common ground with the group of farmers. We are all against the use of eminent domain. We all want clean water. We all hate big corporations, who think they know better and can do whatever they want no matter the consequences to the people. I am a Democrat and am pretty sure the rest of the folks around the table are Republicans, but I did not ask. We were there together that night trying to figure out how to level the playing field for family farmers against a big corporation, selling the idea that we needed them—and only them—to save our small rural towns. That group of farmers and rural citizens is still fighting Costco's massive chicken plant, which is designed to process anywhere from one million to up to two million chickens a day, thus totally displacing family farmers and in essence creating a monopoly on how chickens are raised in Nebraska. They were able to ensure that the plant was not built in Nickerson, Nebraska. However, Costco went to the town next to them and is about to start construction. Without water quality laws in place, Costco just might get what they want: to feed the $5 roasted chicken addiction, all on the backs of our rural communities.

It's not just Costco. In Minnesota, my friend Winona LaDuke is leading the fight for food sovereignty. She is a Native American leader, farmer, pipeline fighter, and water protector. She is working hard to raise awareness about bad corporate actors, including some foreign governments buying up a bunch of land so they can use our natural resources to ship food back to their country. This is happening more and more across the Midwest. China continues to not only buy up food corporations, like Smithfield, but also sew up land. As a country, we could ban this practice while also making sure we are honoring treaties to sovereign tribal nations. Winona is not only stopping risky export pipelines from destroying native rice fields but is also teaching indigenous young people how to grow hemp and other sustainable farming practices. Winona is often in the courts, trying to get land back in the hands of tribal nations. She knows this battle well. The White Earth Nation's original 837,000 acres are now in the hands of non-indigenous individuals. Those who have control of the land control its destiny and control the food and energy created. I've been in many rooms with my friend Winona as she explains the relationship of the land and water. She often closes her talks with this quote: "Ojibwe prophecy speaks of a time during the seventh fire when our people will have a choice between two paths. The first path is well worn and scorched. The second path is new and green. It is our choice as communities and individuals how we will proceed." Winona is strong and powerful. She is transforming the way people across our country see farmers. She can outride any cowboy. She is a rural leader we should all be following.

And in Omaha, Dave Domina, a crusading lawyer who grew up on a farm, is showing the path for legal action against corporate agriculture. While dressed in a suit, he is never seen without his cowboy boots. Domina has an amazing legal record. He successfully sued Tyson on the grounds of cheating family ranchers out of millions through anticompetitive practices. He aided in the impeachment of two Nebraska elected officials. He helped alongside Bold Nebraska and the Nebraska Easement Action Team to keep the Keystone XL Pipeline from touching an ounce of Nebraska's soil with a successful model of uniting family farmers and ranchers in a pact not to sign any contract TransCanada puts in front of them. He is appropriately named David, since the fights he takes on are often against the Goliaths of the world. Domina is known for pulling out a seed bag and going through the lines of fine print an untrained eye would not even notice. On the bag is legal language that boils down to this: Farmers do not control their seed or crop. Companies like Monsanto, which control most seed planted in America, are squeezing out competition to control the market. They are a monopoly and everyone seems to look the other way, just as you would if you were trying to understand the contract on the bag of seed corn. This is a dangerous road we are on as a country.

"Diminishing from our midst is a whole kind of citizen, the citizen who is produced on a farm or ranch. That is the vanishing commodity of American agriculture," Domina told Nick Bergin at the *Lincoln Journal Star*. "It is happening because our production is matching the demand in the marketplaces it sells to. And we are allowing it to consolidate to the point where we don't have kids in rural Nebraska."

Family farms and ranches are rooted in a history of fairness, independence, and grit that was the foundation of vibrant rural communities. Main streets thrived. Seed suppliers, independent meat processors and butchers, local mechanics, farm cooperatives, car and tractor dealerships, and other businesses grew. Our middle class was strong. Now huge multinational corporations and monopolies are taking over and putting immense pressure on our producers and rural communities. We are facing another farm crisis, with 2018 being the fifth year in a row that the average farm did not make a profit. Big corporations are extracting wealth and natural resources out of our communities, and often out of our country altogether. Our rural communities are quickly becoming factory farms for foreign corporations. Family farmers and ranchers lack open and fair markets to sell their goods. As a result, farming has become less about growing food and more about growing industry profits. Bad deals keep family farms in debt. Multinational corporations buy our land. Corporate chains choke production and efficiency. While these issues might be specific to rural America, they resonate with everyone. Democrats should weave these into the story they're telling and the policy solutions they propose.

I've already seen it pop up in the 2020 presidential election. Senator Elizabeth Warren of Massachusetts has a plan for this big issue facing family farmers. In her own words, "Bad decisions in Washington have consistently favored the interests of multinational corporations and big business lobbyists over the interests of family farmers." Her policy proposal, rolled out during the beginning of her presidential run at the Heartland Forum sponsored by Family Farm Action and the Farmers Union, was clear on putting power back in the hands of family farmers and ranchers. Large corporations are gaining control over how and where family farmers and ranchers can grow and sell crops and meat. Just as we need to break up big banks, we need to break up Big Ag to create a level playing field. Warren proposes reforming outdated laws at the Department of Justice that impact how mega-mergers can take place, laws aimed at blocking competition from the little guys. Warren also goes a step further and talks about the need for legislation aimed at permitting farmers to fix their own equipment—the growing movement known as the "Right to Repair." Big corporations, like John Deere, force a farmer to bring their tractor to an authorized dealer to fix it. All farmers want is the right to repair their own equipment or at least to be able to take it to their local repair shop instead of driving hours to an authorized dealer. Farmers end up paying twice as much to get their tractor fixed. If a farmer decides to be a rebel and fix his or her own farm equipment, the warranty on the tractor becomes null and void.

Additionally, policies like country of origin labeling

are supported not only by rural producers but also by urban consumers. As a mom, I want to know my meat was raised in America, and I am willing to pay a little bit more to make that happen. The many years family farmers and ranchers have been pushing for this basic policy show the very large mountain we are climbing even within the Democratic Party to push back against corporate lobbying groups. We can create a food system that cares for the land, water, and critters; it starts with supporting family farmers and ranchers over corporate agriculture.

There are solid steps we can take now, before politicians get involved, to show that Democrats stand with family farmers. State parties, candidates, and grassroots groups can write a Farmer and Rural Bill of Rights for their town and state. Family Farm Action, a group formed to create political power in farm country, wrote the first Farmer's Bill of Rights in Missouri, where the young state party chair and military veteran Stephen Webber took the document all across the state, speaking to groups in sale barns, churches, and community centers on how the Democratic Party sees them, hears them, and is standing up with them. Since Missouri passed the Farmer's Bill of Rights, Democratic parties in other states like Kansas and Nebraska have followed their lead. These foundational statements help spur more dialogue and engagement in rural towns and gives rural people something concrete to point to on how we as Democrats hear them, think about them, and will fight for them.

DURING THE LAST DECADE I HAVE WORKED WITH RURAL COMMUNITIES AND these are the issues that come up over and over again. Democrats are simply not talking enough about them. The bottom line is rural people hate big—that goes for the big banks, Big Ag, Big Pharma, Big Oil—the list goes on and on. Urban progressives hate big, too. We share this common ground. It's a value rooted in fairness. We all want our families, farms, and small businesses to have an equal shot at living the American dream. We need to have one another's backs more and focus on the local issues that rural people are screaming about: protecting the land from big corporations and connecting us all to one another.

KANSAS FARMERS AND RURAL COMMUNITIES BILL OF RIGHTS

The foundation of any society is the ability to grow food, feed people, and generate an economy through agriculture. Accordingly, we believe farmers and rural economies should be protected, maintained, and sustained for the good of all Kansans. The Farmer and Rural Communities Bill of Rights is a renewal of our commitment to the rights of our independent family farmers and ranchers to maintaining fairness, equality, and justice for all concerned.

The Kansas Democratic Party is steadfast in the belief that farmers, ranchers, and rural Kansans are entitled to the following rights:

- **The Right to Fair and Open Markets**, including strong antitrust safeguards, competition between buyers of farm products and those selling to farmers, and protections of contract farmers from multinational corporations.

- **The Right to Feed Our Community** affordably and in a manner that encourages healthy citizens and families.

- **The Right to Fair Capital**, ensuring that family farmers and small businesses can equally access fair credit to invest in the revitalization of their communities.

- **The Right to Protect Our Natural Resources** for generations to come, including the termination and prevention of any corporate stacking and capturing of government agencies, as well as the implementation of meaningful regulations curbing corporate overreach and control.

- **The Right to Local Control of Our Land**, including the termination of foreign corporate ownership of farmland, the protection of a community's right to establish standards for mega-farms, and the limiting of the influence of corporate agribusiness.

- **The Right to Food Security**, because feeding Kansans is a matter of state and national security. A thriving local and regional food system must be maintained to ensure that security.

- **The Right to Repair Our Own Tractors and Equipment** free from predatory contracts that increase operating costs and stifle competition in the equipment service market.

- **The Right to Transparent Labeling** including country of origin labeling and clear, transparent labels for consumers.

- **The Right to Access and Opportunity** in education funding, health care, and hospitals, and the proper public funding of extension offices so that the best and widest array of agricultural policies are available to all Kansans.

- **The Right to a Brighter Future** for the next generation, one of new economic opportunities and access to basic services regardless of location.

4

HOT BUTTONS AND WEDGE ISSUES

I have a few problems with your platform, for one, the Second Amendment.

—CALEB POLLARD, FOUNDER OF
SCRATCHTOWN BREWING COMPANY

emocrats will continue to lose elections in rural states unless we figure out better ways to confront the hot buttons and wedge issues. I am not talking about how we can find a new message or poll-tested phrase that can magically get candidates elected. I am talking about something much simpler (and cheaper!): being authentic. You do not have to wear a Carhartt jacket and twist yourself into a pretzel to become what you think rural voters want to hear and see.

I've always been honest with rural voters that we will not agree on some issues. Instead, I focus on the issues where we are standing together. One thing is abundantly clear: Sticking with the status quo Republican candidates is not the answer. Farmers are living on razor-thin margins, small schools are being forced to close, and health care costs continue to rise. All of this happens when you have one-party rule across rural states. Republicans do not have to address these issues because the Democrats are not investing real resources to win hearts, minds, and elections.

We need to stop letting ourselves be torn apart on these issues. Instead, we need to acknowledge that this is happening, and it is being done to us by Republican political powers. If we stay stuck in these corners, we are not going to solve the problem of climate change, protect our water, or to make sure health care is finally a human right. What we need to do is start to create an authentic relationship with rural voters so we can disagree on issues and still earn their votes.

When a Democratic candidate decides to run in a rural state, a D.C. consultant inevitably says that he or she should avoid talking about "God, gays, and guns." As they told my husband, Scott, when he ran, go meet with the National Rifle Association and seek their endorsement. At the very least, demonstrate that you support the Second Amendment so the NRA doesn't dump millions running against you. Consultants fed Scott lines like "I will stay out of your bedroom if you stay out of my gun closet." Like many rural Democrats, Scott does enjoy going hunting with his friends. He likes shooting sporting clays. He also believes we need gun laws to better protect our kids from endless shootings. All of the advice Democrats in rural states receive around wedge issues often sounds creepy and outdated.

These days, the hot buttons are abortion, immigration, and yes, still guns. Just a few years ago the big hot-button issues would have included gay marriage. Over the years this has changed dramatically across the country, including in rural towns. More and more families have loved ones who are out and not hiding their sexual orientation or gender identity. The massive work done by activists from the ACT UP, Don't Ask, Don't Tell, and gay marriage movements has changed the hearts and minds of people all across the country. Of course there are still major issues facing the LGBT community in our small rural towns, especially for the transgender community, which is facing terrifying violence. When we first moved to Hastings, a total of seven people marched in the Pride Parade. Today that number is over two hundred. But LGBT workers can still be fired for being who they are and loving whom they love in many states across our country.

If we keep listening to the consulting class instead of the people, we will continue to lose rural voters. You cannot avoid the hot-button issues, because people love talking about them. It's kind of like we say we hate reality TV, but there we are watching *The Bachelor* and

The Real Housewives. You do not need a perfectly poll-tested message. If you have that, you will sound like a robot. Rural people know they will not agree with Democrats on every issue. Democrats can start to build the trust, enough to earn the votes of rural people, if we start creating authentic relationships based on common ground.

GUNS

There are few homes in rural America that you will walk into without seeing a Ducks Unlimited sticker, a gun safe, or a deer shed. Men—and yes, plenty of women, too—love spending time hunting or simply shooting clays with family and friends. Rural folks view guns differently than people in urban areas do. First, we see them as carrying on a family tradition—in fact, so much so that rifles are often passed down through generations. I know many rural folks who have their great-grandfather's rifle and memories of hunting with family members. Second, we see them as necessary to protect our families in remote areas where police could be an hour away. Third, the reality is, sometimes predators need to be shot or they will eat the livestock being raised. The Second Amendment is how folks describe gun rights in rural communities. It is a fundamental freedom enshrined in our Constitution. When rural people look at a gun, they see a rite of passage, tradition, hunting, safety, and plain old fun with their buddies.

There is common ground to be found on guns. Some of it can be built around an already existing deep skepticism that many rural Americans have toward the NRA. That might be surprising for blue state Democrats to hear, but the NRA has become a big corporate lobbying group that cares more about gun manufacturers than about protecting the Second Amendment. One farmer told me he would never join the NRA because "If I am worried about the government truly coming to take my guns, the NRA has the biggest list of gun owners with their members." Instead, most gun owners I know are members of Ducks Unlimited and Pheasants Forever, bird conservation organizations that offer gun safety classes in small towns and a strong message of protecting the land and wildlife habitat. These groups also cook a mean prime rib with cheesy potatoes at their annual dinners. One of the first events I went to in Nebraska was a Ducks Unlimited dinner where I got a bottle of Jack Daniel's with a duck band (used to track birds for conservation purposes) that I still wear proudly as a ring every day.

After a meeting one night about Costco's massive chicken barns encroaching on family farmers, one of the guys says I can follow him into town for a county board meeting. I get in my minivan and follow his pickup truck. On the back of his truck is a Tea Party bumper sticker talking about freedom and another one with a picture of a pencil and the words: "If a gun kills people, then a pencil misspells words." As we drive down the dirt roads to get into town, I wonder if he will bring up guns. As I get out of the car, he comes up to me and says, "So what do you think of my bumper stickers." I smile at him, throw my arm around his shoulder, give a little chuckle, and say, "We do not agree on guns, but I am here and we do agree on clean water and property rights, so let's start there." He smiled back and said, "Well, all right." We then started to walk toward the fire station, which was packed with rural folks from the town. The room was so overcrowded that someone had opened the windows and people had pulled their pickups next to the building so people could sit in the beds of the trucks to hear the meeting. A small town was standing up to a big corporation that night, and they won. The commissioners sided with the citizens and told Costco to go find somewhere else that would buy their weaselly sales pitch. We did not agree on gun rights that night, but I did show that a Democrat stands with them on issues critical to their livelihoods.

We need more of these moments—more Democrats standing with communities on our shared values and helping to highlight the issues they are facing. If I had said to the farmer that he was wrong on guns and his bumper stickers were stupid, where would that have put us? How would that move any conversation forward? I had the reverse experience happen as well in the rural town of Ord, where Caleb Pollard, the owner of the Scratchtown Brewing Company, was invited to address our state central committee meeting of the Nebraska Democratic Party. I try as chair of the party to bring in speakers from the communities we are visiting. We travel around the state to hold our meetings, thus ensuring that both rural and urban towns see us and get a few more dollars in their local economy's pocket. Caleb was talking about guns and the Second Amendment when he started to get yelled at by some folks from Omaha, who had, rightfully so, different opinions on guns. Caleb is an independent. He is young. He is raising his family in the small rural town of Ord, population 2,103. He should really be mayor of the town, and he supports more clean energy and more green spaces. He also knows there is a role for government in revitalizing our small towns. But the moment he brought up guns, the divisions and walls went up. This is what the Republican Party is counting on—that we stay divided.

If you have an opportunity to go hunting, you should. Senator Chuck Schumer, a New Yorker through and through, once joined former senator Ben Nelson on a pheasant hunt in Nebraska. While hunting, they talked about health care policy and Schumer got to see beautiful parts of rural Nebraska. Schumer ended up being a good shot and bagged a few birds. I don't know for sure, but

I am guessing this was the first and last time Schumer picked up a gun. I went hunting with my husband and his friends. First, they told me I was not dressed properly—I had on UGGs, jeans, and some cute puffy vest I bought in D.C. years ago. Then there was my endless list of questions. And then . . . well, let's just say I was not a good shot like Senator Schumer. Instead they literally had to shake a tree in hopes a pheasant would be in my shooting range, and when it was, I swung my gun around and all the guys hit the ground. Needless to say, I have not been invited to go hunting again.

As a mom, I am terrified of school shootings. Schools should be a safe place, plain and simple. When school started this year, I started to see ads about bulletproof backpacks. Our kids are going through drills in case of a school shooter. This is not supposed to be our kids' experiences. I want to see stronger gun laws. I also want to make sure we do not demonize gun owners. Let's set our sights on the NRA and the politicians beholden to it and get some commonsense protections in place so folks can hunt and our kids are safe. There is common ground between urban and rural voters on gun policies. We all want to see background checks for guns, including those purchased at gun shows. We believe anyone on the no-fly list should also be on a no-buy list for guns. We think anyone with a record of violence should not have access to firearms. We should not be arming teachers. We agree the NRA is just another lobbying group looking out for big corporations and no longer represents the hunters across America.

Here's an idea supported by many grassroots individuals like Melody Vaccaro, who started the group Nebraskans Against Gun Violence. We need to require liability insurance on all gun purchases and gun manufacturers. Once that happens, you actually will see laws getting in place, because now there is a tangible, enforceable financial interest for safety. The only way we can get to this solution is repealing the national law that protects the gun industry from civil lawsuits.

For generations we have talked about the need for gun safety laws, and the NRA has been able to buy off enough politicians to keep the status quo. We have witnessed first-graders killed in classrooms and families in prayer being murdered in church. No one needs a weapon of war to go hunting. Rural people know this and agree. As Democrats, we have to remain firm and push for gun reform and not let mailers from the NRA stop us from doing what is right and building on the common ground the majority of Americans hold on this issue.

ABORTION

When you drive down rural roads, you will end up seeing many pro-life billboards. Over the years, I have noticed that there are fewer and fewer, and many are fading in the sun. However, they are still a fixture in rural towns just as much as a big red barn. In Nebraska, 60 percent of the voters are pro-life, while that same number believes abortion should remain legal. I can see you shaking your head. I get it. But the reality is, many pro-life voters also stand with Democrats in keeping abortion legal. We are talking past each other.

I was raised in a pro-life home. My mom was president of the Broward County Right to Life chapter. I made posters, marched, attended prayer vigils, and helped my mom set up booths at county fairs. I understand the pro-life movement through my mom's eyes. She got pregnant at eighteen and understood that young pregnant women needed help of all kinds, from buying formula to obtaining clothes and housing. My mom, like many pro-life voters, has a deeply personal reason she is pro-life. She looks at my sister, who she had at eighteen years old, and could never see herself as anything but pro-life. My mom, still a registered Republican, has voted for Democrats since 2008 and volunteered for Hillary Clinton's run for president.

All of this may sound impossible and hypocritical. I have heard all the arguments and talking points plenty of times. "If you think abortion should remain legal, than you are pro-choice." "You need to stop using the term *pro-life* and use *anti-choice*." "No candidate should be welcome in the Democratic Party if they are pro-life."

Staying with these talking points will not bring rural voters to our party and will not win over pro-life voters. Some people call themselves pro-life for emotional and religious reasons. It is part of who they are, a fundamental identity. Fighting and arguing about one's identity will lead us nowhere fast. Instead we need to look for areas where we can help women and children.

Democrats are in a better position than Republicans to make the case for expanding Medicaid, which helps kids grow up healthy and helps pregnant women get the care they need. Democrats defend funding for Title X, which is government funding that helps women and men get access to birth control, the number one way we can reduce the amount of abortions happening in our country. Democrats support comprehensive sex education that teaches our kids how to respect their bodies and stay safe and reduce pregnancies in teens. All of this is tied to access to health care and the fundamental rights of women.

Republicans use abortion to divide us and to keep us divided. Republicans have ruled in red states for decades and hammer on this issue in order to keep winning elections. Democrats, instead of saying Republicans are using this as a wedge issue out loud, ask pollsters and consultants to help them craft a message that will both keep pro-choice voters at the table and pass enough with pro-life voters to win the election. This approach is totally wrong. It is not authentic, and it is one of the reasons why Democrats are losing. There are single-issue voters who will never change and never vote for a Democrat who wants to ensure that abortion remains safe and legal. Those voters we will not reach, and those voters are not in the majority.

As Democrats, we need to be honest about where we stand on the issue of abortion, tell our story on why we hold our beliefs, and then also talk about policies to protect women and children. A Democrat running for mayor in Nebraska was faced with this very issue in 2017. Heath Mello is a strong Democrat who helped pass major laws to help Dreamers and unions; he is also pro-life. He got pulled into a national debate on whether the Democratic Party should allow pro-life candidates at the table after the 2016 loss to Trump. What happened to Heath was unfair. The chair of the Democratic National Committee (DNC), Tom Perez, issued a press release targeted at Heath saying pro-life Democrats are not welcome in our party, even though Joe Biden, Tim Kaine, and several other prominent Democrats describe themselves as pro-life and also say they would never restrict a women's right to abortion. Neither Heath nor I got a phone call from the DNC to discuss this at all. I learned about it in the parking lot at Walgreens, when a reporter called me. All of this was extremely frustrating because on the ground Heath was supported by numerous board members of Planned Parenthood.

Instead of telling his story, Heath tried to avoid the issue that was dominating headlines from the *Omaha World-Herald* to *The Nation* magazine. Heath was adopted and raised by a mom who cleaned houses to make sure he had everything he needed as a kid. He is a practicing Catholic with two children. Heath worked to get Republicans to compromise on a bill that would have required a woman to look at a sonogram image before she got an abortion. Heath worked to make that optional for the woman. Heath had a story to tell; however, like most Democrats, we wanted to avoid talking about the personal and controversial issue of abortion. He lost his race.

I described myself as pro-life until my early twenties, when a friend of mine had an abortion. She knew I was pro-life and did not come to me when she needed me the most because she was terrified of my judging her and not supporting her. That fact hit me like a ton of bricks. Here was someone I loved and shared everything with, and she thought I would not support her. I started to see the other side of a deeply personal issue. She was one of the first people in her family to go to college and knew she would have to drop out to be closer to her parents. She made the decision that was best for her. Who was I—or anyone else, for that matter—to judge or second-guess her? This is also true for women who choose to have a baby.

Women are simply better equipped to be making the laws around access to abortion and birth control.

Women themselves have to face the consequences of the decision one way or another. Many women have had an abortion and later become a mom. We see and understand both decisions. I'm one of those women. In my late twenties, while I was in graduate school in D.C., I was a single mom. I chose to have an abortion years earlier, when I lived in Tallahassee during my first job out of college. Both decisions were right for me. When I was a single mom living in D.C., I brought my daughter Kora to class with me because affordable day care was not an option. When I had to take time off work to have Kora, I also had to go on the Special Supplemental Nutrition Program for Women, Infants, and Children (WIC), a USDA program, so I had access to formula and food to keep us both healthy. In other words, the government stepped in when I needed some help. Democrats support WIC. Democrats support reforming child care in concrete ways like expanding public schools to start at age three for all kids, not just kids in Head Start and those with learning disabilities. Our middle child, Maya, did not speak until she was about age three, and without the support of the public schools in our small town, she would not have been the avid reader she is today. All kids should have access to early education. Democrats also support fully paid parental leave. As a party, the Democrats support women and children in concrete ways, not just the lip service Republicans give us around election time. We have firm ground to talk to pro-life voters, and we should stop trying to hide or cede this ground to Republicans.

I often wonder why national Republicans didn't take federal action on abortion in 2017 or 2018. Donald Trump is supposedly pro-life and Republicans had majorities in both the House and the Senate. The answer is simple. They didn't take action because if they did, they would not have a major fundraising pitch and issue to wedge rural and urban voters. This is not to say women's reproductive health is not under a serious threat right now. It is. There are draconian reproductive laws being passed all over the country. We should fight them in the streets and in the courts. We must also call out the Republican Party for using abortion as a single issue to win elections. They do not want to resolve this issue. Because if they did, we would see massive investments in comprehensive sex education programs and access to free birth control. Those are the programs that reduce abortions. The laws Republicans are passing will not reduce abortions. The laws Republicans are passing will kill women. And quite frankly, they should be forced to sign the death certificates of all the women their reckless laws will kill.

We need to stop this endless fight. We need to welcome voters who identify as pro-life into the Democratic Party. We need to make it clear you can be pro-life and still uphold laws that protect women's reproductive rights. We need to ensure women have access to safe and legal abortions in every state. We need to be honest with voters on how the Republican Party uses abortion as an issue to divide and conquer rather than bring people together and solve issues facing women and children, like access to health care. We need to tell our stories about why we are pro-life or pro-choice and acknowledge we all have diverse and different backgrounds and that is what makes us stronger. We also need to hear the stories of others with different views on abortion even when we disagree and not cast judgment on them. Talking past one another will not help women. Talking past one another allows Republicans to callously use this deeply personal issue to win elections rather than support women and families.

IMMIGRATION

President Trump campaigned on the promise to build a wall that Mexico would pay for. The wall would keep America safe and keep criminals and drugs out of our country, and this was necessary, according to Trump and his ilk, because "Mexicans are animals, drug dealers, and rapists." The wall was in many ways the perfect symbol for the fears and insecurities of families living paycheck to paycheck or working in dead-end jobs. Yet the comments I hear while I am having a beer with some farmers or waiting in line at the grocery store convince me that rural folks know the wall is a dumb idea and a total waste of money. The fact that rural voters know this and still vote for Trump reflects our failure as Democrats to speak to the fears we all have about economic insecurity. In small and rural towns all over the country, immigrants are breathing life into our schools, churches, and communities.

The face of rural communities is mostly white, but not only white. There are Native Americans, African Americans, Latinos, Asian Americans, and immigrants of all backgrounds in rural communities. In fact, some of Nebraska's small towns like Schuyler are now over 70 percent Latino. Nationally, in rural towns, communities of color make up about 20 percent of the population, and it is rising. Families come to rural towns for jobs, for the low cost of living, and for the feeling of safety in these small communities. The changes do cause some to be uncomfortable, and there is racism in rural and urban communities all across our country. There are also welcoming communities and relationships being formed, which were on full display when ICE raided several businesses in the small rural town of O'Neill, Nebraska. The school's superintendent opened the school's doors to make sure kids whose parents had just been handcuffed and placed on a bus were taken care of by local residents. Lawyers from the cities came up to help provide legal assistance.

The churches in town prepared food. Businesses are still closed because of the raids. Families are still torn apart. The kids involved will undoubtedly never forget the trauma, but they will also hopefully remember the teachers, religious leaders, and neighbors who came to make sure they were safe. The raids meant fewer kids at the already struggling rural school and no local workforce, which forced the tomato processing plant to bus in workers. Bryan Corkle, a teacher and wrestling coach, told the *Lincoln Journal Star*, "Where we used to have families of immigrants, and families who were involved in school and sent kids to school, now we have folks who are bused into our community and are living in a hotel. Tell me how our community benefited?"

As Democrats, we need to push back on Trump's cruelty toward women, children, and families who are coming to America for a better life. Watching what is happening at the border is hard for most Americans. We feel hopeless and helpless in the face of babies being torn from their mom and dads. The stories about the lack of basic showers and food on our watch are incomprehensible, especially for the Republican Party members, who often drape themselves in Christianity. In all my years of Catholic school, I never once heard Sister Mary Ann or any of the priests telling me I should turn my back on people who are in need. We need to protest in the streets. We need to donate to grassroots groups like the Refugee and Immigrant Center for Education and Legal Services (RAICES) and national groups like the American Civil Liberties Union (ACLU), who are fighting every single day to protect children and keep families together. We also need to listen to the stories of immigrant families who are building up our rural and red states.

Scott and I attended a friend's birthday party and were talking with Orlando, the father of Dulce, who just got a full scholarship to a university in a rural Nebraska town to become a physician's assistant. It's a grant program a few universities have in our state as a way to keep rural young people home. We need to invest more money in such programs all over the country. Orlando said something to me that made me think that we are approaching immigration all wrong, simply because we have failed to ask immigrant families to be a part of the local solution rather than seeing this purely as a national policy fix. He said to me, "We feel forgotten. No one sees us. The politicians do not talk to us. They do not ask us what is needed. We are working hard every single day and no one is here for us." Talk about a gut punch. His oldest son is a Dreamer, and Dulce was born in America. Orlando is undocumented. Orlando works seven days a week to provide for his family. He feels left behind, just like a lot of rural people. Donald Trump might have activated a racist branch of the American family tree, but he also is energizing undocumented and new American citizens and those of us standing with them—those of us who see Orlando and Dulce as our friends and as critical parts of the community. Nebraska is Orlando's home. America is Orlando's home. Orlando has lived and worked in America for thirty years. He has employed dozens of workers. He pays taxes. He does not take and is not eligible for any government programs. Rural America is being revitalized with immigrant families. As Democrats, we have to show up for them. It is not enough to be outraged by Trump's inhumane policies.

We need to take a policy lesson from President Ronald Reagan and Speaker of the House Tip O'Neill. In the late 1980s, Reagan worked with Democrats to provide a path to citizenship for undocumented immigrants living and working in America. Instead of welcoming immigrants wanting to make their lives better and contribute to America, we are now turning people into villains. Why can't we just get back to the basics again? Ensure that every immigrant who is in America undocumented becomes an American citizen. We also need to ensure that there are limits to the numbers of immigrants coming to America in the future so we have clear rules of the road. The immigration law passed by Reagan did not have a clear pathway to citizenship, something all countries need to figure out fast so families are not waiting ten to twenty years to become American citizens.

There are many Republican voters from Mexico, Guatemala, and El Salvador, who became citizens under Reagan's immigration policy. They saw a political party standing up for them, and they in turn stood with the party. Ron Rivera, a second-generation American working at the Nebraska Democratic Party, described to me his father's loyalty to the Republicans. "My dad sees more opportunities in the Republican Party. He was raised in a religious home. Growing up, I watched my dad's opinion on issues and realized I did not agree with him. The funny thing is, I was named after Ronald Reagan. My dad worked hard to make sure we had food on the table and we could get a good education. He came to this country for the reason everyone does, for better opportunity and more freedom. My values lined up with the Democratic Party, but I got involved in politics because of volunteering on a ballot campaign against the death penalty with my best friend. Democrats reached out to me when I was an Independent and did not look at me like I did not have anything to offer. I just want to help others do better in life. I want people to have opportunities."

Listening to Ron reinforces a lot of lessons for our party, from making sure we are reaching out to young people and Independents to keeping the basic tenet of being the party of hope, not fear, in our messaging. Above and beyond this, though, is our need to recruit new Americans to run for office in rural communities. We need more rural people, period, in all levels of our

Democratic Party leadership. I deeply believe electing more Americans representing communities of color is a clear and concrete way to demonstrate where our immigration policies stand today. Above all the other policy positions and ideas we have put out there on immigration, which are solid and should be acted on, we need to change the face of politics. When we have more Latino and Asian and African and Middle Eastern rural Americans elected at the local and state level, working as elected officials on the local issues from school lunches to potholes, we will start to confront racism and stereotypes. When we are all working together during school board and city council meetings, when we are in the weeds on local issues, that is when we finally see one another as people living in rural towns wanting to make life better for our families instead of allowing ourselves to be divided against one another.

When we welcome communities of color coming to small towns for jobs and quality of life, it changes all of us, makes us see life in different ways. This is a good thing. Schools that were at risk of closing are now filled with kids. Storefronts on main streets that were boarded up are now selling food, clothes, and furniture. Meatpacking plants have reopened, and the line workers that used to be Irish and Polish immigrants are now Mexican, Guatemalan, and Sudanese immigrants. America is changing. Rural communities faces are changing. As

Democrats, we have to stand with rural towns and not write them off. As immigrants become citizens, we have to be there to help them understand the electoral process. My mind was blown when I learned that many new citizens went to polling stations and were shocked they could not vote. They assumed because they were now American citizens that they also could vote. They did not realize there was a registration process you had to follow in order to vote. The only way we can make sure more voters have the power to change elections is being in the rural towns and organizing shoulder to shoulder with the communities—not telling them what to do, but rather listening and being their allies.

We cannot be played against one another and bullied by the Republican Party on the issue of immigration. We are a nation of immigrants. We are a nation that understands right and wrong. It's wrong to separate families. Jimmy Carter used to say, "Every day we are given pieces of wood. Whether we build a wall or a bridge is up to us." Locally, this is all up to us. We have no other option but to make sure people like Orlando have a clear set of rules to become a citizen. It should not include "going back home to the back of the line and wait his turn" or continuing to be in limbo as he fights for the American Dream every day. We need to support more college programs like the one Dulce is participating in so she can go to college in rural America and give back to our rural towns as a nurse. We need to reach out to welcome into our party young people like Ron Rivera, who could have followed his dad into the Republican Party but instead is shaping Democratic politics at the local and state level. We need to change the face of our Democratic Party.

5

ORGANIZING AND REBUILDING THE DEMOCRATIC PARTY IN RURAL AMERICA

Nothing changes until someone is made to feel uncomfortable.

—FRANK LAMERE

When I was little, I created membership cards for my friends to play hide-and-go-seek. A little extreme for eight-year-olds, yeah. But what can I say? Action and organizing is in my DNA. I want to end this book with concrete ideas that grassroots activists, candidates, elected officials, and the Democratic Party can take to bridge the rural and urban divide and start to listen to and win back rural voters.

My husband, Scott, ran for Congress in one of the most conservative districts in the nation (to say we both love a challenge is an understatement). At one of the campaign stops, an old-timer raised his hand and went on to say, "You know, I've been back here listening to what you're saying and I'm agreeing with most of it—more of it than I thought, to be honest. My friend thought it'd be a laugh to come tonight, and then he didn't come. But dammit, I've just been wondering why the hell I'm a Republican if I agree with you this much. And then it finally dawned on me. I'm a religious guy—well, I mean I believe in God. That's about it, except I also think I should go to church if I believe in God, so I do. And it hit me. If Hemingford had only one church in town, guess what denomination I'd be? Whatever the hell that church was! I've never met a Democrat, so I'm a Republican. So anyway, I guess I don't really have a question but I'll sure as hell vote for ya. Thanks, that's it. Sorry to take everyone's time."

I hear comments like this all over the country no matter what rural community I am in, whether it is on the coasts, in the South, on the Plains, or in the West. Democrats have been absent from rural communities for decades. So much so, you have good, strong Democrats who say they whisper to their friends or coworkers "I am a Democrat, too," when the subject comes up. It's not necessarily that rural people think they will lose their job if they proudly proclaim they are a Democrat, it's more about a rural culture of not wanting to rock the boat and wanting to get along. And in a small town, you see everyone at the coffee shop, grocery store, kids' soccer games, and church. Adding in a political divide just makes it uncomfortable. Generations go by with no investments from the Democratic Party to win elections, and you get where we are at this moment. A place where rural people agree with us on major issues from confronting climate change to public education to the rising costs of health care and the fundamental belief that big corporations have more power than the people. But they are not yet voting for Democratic candidates.

Over the years I have learned a few things about how the Democratic Party and how major donors work. During my time working as the executive director of the Young Democrats of America, we pushed our party to invest and reach out to young voters. We had to make the case, because most of the Democratic leaders told us the same thing every time we went into a meeting with our plan, "Why would we give you money? Young people do not vote." We were lucky to have a donor, Jonathan Lewis, and his political advisor, Paul Yandura, who did not listen to the D.C. insiders and instead bet on us underdog young people who had clear ideas to turn around the youth vote decline. Democrats who believe in rural voters are walking a familiar path to make the case to those with access to resources to invest in rural voters, red state parties, and red state candidates. I hope the outcome is the same. When the Democratic Party started to invest real money into targeting and turning out young voters, we saw record increases in the youth vote. Indeed, they were margin of victory for many campaigns around the country. I deeply believe rural voters can be the margin of victory for Democrats. Thus we can start to elect more rural candidates at the local, state, and federal level, making our party stronger.

As Democrats, we can move forward in bridging the rural and urban divide as well as in having more rural voices being heard within the Democratic Party. When you work with rural people, you begin to see a different side of rural people and you start to look at issues with a different lens. None of these suggestions for the Democratic Party mean we should stop funding blue and purple states, nor should we stop supporting all the great new resistance groups like Swing Left or Indivisible, which have popped up in mostly urban and suburban areas. We need all of what we are currently investing in to win elections. We also need to be truly honest and recognize we will not win statewide races unless we start to close the gap with rural voters. Our policies will be better with both an urban and a rural presence at the table. Shirley Chisholm told women: "If they don't give you a seat at the table, bring a folding chair." In that same spirit, it is time for us to bring an entire bench's worth of people from rural America, each with a hot dish and lots of strong opinions. Doing so will make all of us uncomfortable. We will make mistakes and will get frustrated with one another. The late Frank LaMere, the longest-serving Native American on the DNC, would often say, "Nothing changes until someone is made to feel uncomfortable." We need to change and reform and rebuild our party. We need rural, suburban, and urban voters at the table. If we hide in our corners, nothing will move forward.

SHOW UP IN RURAL TOWNS WITH A MEGAPHONE

Rural communities are ignored and forgotten by Democrats and taken for granted by Republicans. We change this by showing up. One of the loudest voices for years on how the Democratic Party can reach rural America is Tom Vilsack, the former secretary of agriculture and two-term governor of Iowa. He wrote in *Democracy* about how candidates and the party leaders need to show up with solutions and ideas on issues but also how we must push back on how Republicans divide us. He said, "Democrats offered little to rebut the Republican mantra of a government that was inefficient, ineffective, and rife with fraud, waste, and abuse. We provided no real pushback to the notion that people would be better off with less government or a tax system that favored the wealthy while squeezing the middle class."

Willie Nelson, Reverend William Barber, Representative Tim Ryan, Senator Tester, and Winona LaDuke are all national leaders putting a spotlight on rural issues. So are less famous people like Matt Hildreth, Laurie

Bertram Roberts, Rion Ramirez, Liberty Schneider, Chris Reeves, and Yolanda Nuncio. Every single one of these leaders works with rural communities, both with farmers and ranchers as well as diverse communities in rural towns. When you show up in rural towns, you are showing you care about the people, the land, and the way of life so many of us love and are working to protect. Candidates from urban communities do not need to stress out about saying the wrong thing or getting lost on a dirt road. Rural people want to talk about our towns. We want to share how the hospital is on its last leg. We want to brag about the young person who served in the military and came home to open a brewery. If you remember the lesson I quickly learned that you have two ears and one mouth for a reason, you will be just fine.

INVEST IN RED STATE PARTIES, CANDIDATES, AND GRASSROOTS GROUPS

Chloe Maxmin and her campaign manager, Canyon Woodward, decided to take on what others would say is impossible: to run, at the age of twenty-six, in rural Maine in a deeply conservative district. She believed in the people and deployed grassroots organizing tactics of training volunteers and going door to door. Chloe and Canyon wrote about their campaign in *The Nation*, starting the article with a story familiar to us organizers and

Democratic Party leaders in red and rural states. Chloe walked up a dirt road to a trailer. Most folks would have kept on walking by, making all the wrong assumptions about people living inside, including that they are not registered and they do not care about politics. She knocked on the door and engaged in a conversation with a voter, who told her she was the first politician who had ever come to his house and listened to him. She earned his vote. I hear this type of story over and over again when I talk to rural candidates and state party chairs. I was told once when I spoke at a Democratic county meeting that I was the first party leader to come visit with them since the 1970s. Chloe sums it up pretty well on the task ahead: "The left abandoned rural America, leaving its citizens behind. Our campaign shows that building true representational political power requires investing in state-level politics that translate progressive values to the realities of rural America and revive faith in local political movements."

Just ten years ago, in Nebraska and in many rural communities across the country, Democrats were losing rural communities with a twenty-point margin, still giving statewide and presidential candidates a shot to win. Today we are losing with a forty-point margin, and there are simply not enough votes in the urban centers to make up for that gap. We have excellent candidates and a great message, but they have no resources. You cannot win elections, especially statewide and federal ones, without money no matter how great your candidate is or how strong a message he or she is carrying.

In the beginning of every election cycle, the Democratic Party and all the campaign committees that support candidates look at the raw numbers and put resources into so-called swing states, where the gap between Democratic and Republican voter registration is less than ten points. Occasionally there will be a bright star candidate that gets the attention of the Democratic Party, but generally, rural candidates are left off the list—a list also given to major donors across the country—of candidates everyone is to invest in for that cycle. I know plenty of great candidates from red states who tell me that when they finally get in front of major donors, they all get the same message: "When you get on the DCCC red-to-blue list, give me a call. Maybe then I will consider giving to you."

Not only is this happening to candidates, it is also happening to state parties, which are the backbone to campaigns across the country. We have state parties that are running with no paid staff. Over half of the state party chairs are unpaid volunteer positions, and the overwhelming majority of those are in, you guessed it, red states. Can you imagine any other institution that is expected to perform every year with a volunteer CEO, never knowing if they will have any paid staff to get tasks done?

The current Democratic National Committee chair, Tom Perez, made major strides to begin to fix the problem when he got elected after the stinging loss of Hillary Clinton. He recently hired a rural outreach director, Liberty Schneider, who has a long career working in and lifting up rural communities. She hit the ground running, holding trainings online and on the phone with rural DNC members and supporting the Rural Caucus with polling and messaging. Liberty is planning trips to the states and territories to learn about specific rural areas across the country and to help state parties build and rural candidates win.

Chair Perez also heard loud and clear from the state parties that he needed to rebuild the state infrastructure on the ground. The DNC is now giving each state party—no matter if they are in a red, blue, or purple state—$10,000 each month to help pay for core staff and operations. The $10,000 is still far less than what the DNC gave to state parties under Howard Dean, the DNC chair from 2005 to 2009, who invested roughly $25,000 a month in each state party. The investments under Dean paid off at the state and local level—record numbers of Democrats were elected during those years. The recruitment and training of volunteers, the gathering of voter data, and the development of party leaders and a strong campaign staff all happened as a result of Dean's investments.

It was known as the fifty-state strategy, an idea and program developed by state party chairs under the leadership of Ray Buckley, an old-school Democrat from New

Hampshire who knows the value state parties bring to the DNC and candidates. Ray knew the model of targeting only swing states would end in constant failure. To this day, Ray continues to be a reformer in the party pushing for more resources to all states, especially the red and rural ones. He is joined by the current president of the Association of State Democratic Committees (ASDC), Ken Martin from Minnesota. Both Ken and Ray know our state parties are made up of some of the best donors, volunteers, and opinion leaders, who can help candidates navigate the counties and state. The role of the ASDC is to share best practices among state party leaders and to be a voice for the states in the larger DNC family. The organization is underfunded and underappreciated. They also hold the majority of votes on the DNC and were able to stop really bad ideas in recent years—like privatizing our state's voter files. Ken Martin is one of the most impressive and dedicated leaders in the DNC structure right now. He advocates for the states. Ken appreciates leaders like me who deeply believe in the institution and at the same time want to reform the areas I know are holding us back from winning in red and rural states. It should be no surprise that Ken Martin worked with and learned under Senator Paul Wellstone, who believed so strongly that our party is made up of people on the ground. The state parties and grassroots Democrats are Ken's entire driving motivation as he rebuilds the party.

The fifty-state strategy is one of the many reasons President Obama was elected in 2008, outperforming in red states and in rural communities. You would think, then, that under President Obama state parties would be well funded and the fifty-state strategy would go even deeper into red and rural states as well as the seven U.S. territories, which to this day are not funded. This is not what happened. Under President Obama's leadership of the Democratic National Committee, where he got to choose who the chair would be rather than have a robust election, state parties got only $2,500 a month—just a tenth of what they got under Howard Dean. While President Obama was one of the most inspiring and effective presidents, he did not invest in the party infrastructure. Instead, he focused on building the outside group he founded called Organizing for America. This is understandable—it's easier for an outside organization to stay targeted on the president's agenda. Plus, he saw the DNC as an obstacle during his protracted primary with Hillary Clinton in 2007–2008. The DNC largely did not welcome reformers like Obama and his massive network of new volunteers, a problem still lingering today.

Turning around the party and rebuilding it across the country will not be easy. The party apparatus is a large institution with thousands of stakeholders who get elected at the local level. It moves more slowly and is often viewed as too complex from the outside. However, the DNC and state parties are accountable to grass-roots Democrats. If you do not like the direction of the state party, you can mobilize and organize people to get elected to the state convention and vote in new leaders. Not having to deal with that infrastructure and layers of leadership is a plus in the minds of many major donors and party operatives. The big investments in outside groups like Center for American Progress and America Votes, with a large and coordinated donor structure at the Democracy Alliance, meant state parties had more competition for political donations, which are hard to come by since donors do not get tax deductions for the large checks. This competition over the past decade did not drive creativity, which is what some donors thought would happen. It resulted in a massive loss of over 1,200 elected seats in state legislatures all across our country during President Obama's two terms. When you have a turnover that large, it is also hard to start winning state-wide and presidential elections again because of the lack of investment, smaller staffs, and less organization. State parties are the only organizations in every state with the legal structure, institutional knowledge, and mission to elect Democrats. But, without money, you can only push a boulder up a hill for so long.

Investing in state parties is not sexy or some brilliant new idea. We have a program here in Nebraska called Block Captains where volunteers are assigned fifty houses in their neighborhood to talk to voters three times a year. It's effective grassroots work, and volunteers have a ton of fun visiting with their neighbors. Research by leaders such as David Nickerson shows us over and over again that authentic, person-to-person contact is the most effective way to turn out voters. I understand that a program like this one might not be on the top of the list of things major donors and national leaders find intriguing or innovative. Yet it's exactly these types of state party initiatives that help win elections. These functions build the infrastructure. You cannot just plop in a candidate and expect magic to happen. We can't bank on once-in-a-generation talent like a Kennedy or an Obama to magically appear to energize voters. It takes hard work and organization to win elections. For the majority of candidates you need strong county parties and a well-funded state party to help a candidate know where the vote centers are, when the local parades happen, and who the major donors are in the state. You need an active and trained volunteer base. You need local opinion leaders who can endorse your campaign. You need a voter file that identifies who supports Medicaid expansion, who votes only in the presidential years, and who will need more door knocks to get them to turn out for the midterm elections. This is where state parties come in. We know our communities, our civic structures, and our voters. We know our workhorse organizers, our grassroots fundraisers, and even the budding talent. Investing in us should be valued the same as investing in other groups. State parties elect Democrats, plain and simple. And yet, too many state parties do not have the funds to operate on all cylinders.

Laurie Bertram Roberts is the executive director of Mississippi Reproductive Freedom Fund. Running an organization that focuses on reproductive health in a red and rural state is not easy, Laurie understands building power in our rural towns and red states will not happen overnight and that it will take real long-term investments, not just in a targeted race six months before the election. As she puts it: "If you want to win in red states, you have to invest in red state grassroots organizing before elections happen. People need to stop throwing money at organizations at the last minute, expecting we can work miracles, when any other day we're mostly ignored for large national groups. Stop nickel-and-diming us and invest in our work so we have the capacity and infrastructure to really go out and mobilize the base we've grown through doing our work. People smell fake, especially in red states. Country folks can't stand transactional politics. It's why social wedge issues keep working over saying we can do XYZ to improve your life. True organizing takes time, and it's not always measurable on a spreadsheet. Sometimes it's just being in a community [and] getting to know people. That takes money and time, not end-game push dollars, which are great but not what's going to build long-term change."

I will forever stay on my soapbox, saying over and over again that the best bang for your buck is to fund the state parties, especially those of us in red and rural states who know how to stretch a dollar. The cost of a week of TV in Denver or Philadelphia can keep a candidate on the air for a month in rural states. We cannot run our state parties on shoestrings and duct tape and expect different results. We need to change our funding models and change them fast. To be clear, I am not saying one should come at the expense of another. We have a three-legged stool to get good Democratic candidates elected that care about the people. One leg is the party infrastructure, one is outside grassroots groups, and the other is the candidates themselves. We need all three funded, all over the country, in all fifty states, including the seven U.S. territories.

Let me end this section with an example I used to give donors when making the case to invest in young voters. Think about Nike putting out a new sneaker. They do zero marketing. They put nothing on social media. They get no opinion leaders to talk up the sneaker. Then, no one buys the sneaker. Do you really think Nike would blame the customer? No. They would blame their staff and their infrastructure for not reaching out to consumers. The same principle applies to voters and our state parties. If we are not funding our major infrastructure in the states so they can talk to voters, we will continue to lose elections in red and rural states. You cannot blame the voter.

PUT RURAL DEMOCRATS IN LEADERSHIP ROLES

To understand the gap between urban and rural ideas at the national level, you can look at the leadership roles in our Democratic Party committees, specifically the Democratic National Committee. Among the national DNC officers, we have strong leaders like Maria Elena Durazo, who brings labor and migrant workers to the table, and Karen Carter Peterson, bringing black voices to her role in protecting elections. However, we do not have a single rural leader as a DNC officer. Even among other leadership posts in the DNC, caucus, and committee chairs, you will find very few rural leaders.

We need to reform the way we are electing positions within the DNC and other party structures. A major step we should take is to implement a new rule of geographic diversity in our leadership roles within the party so we have more rural voices at the table as decisions are made for programs, messaging, and funding. Trust me, if Senator Tester had been in the room when the Green New Deal talking points were drafted, you would have never seen the "joke" about farting cows. Or, if a rural leader was in the room when Chair Perez was drafting the policies around debates, we could have flagged how the rules hurt rural candidates like Governor Bullock, who simply do not have the ability to hit those higher numbers unless people start to see him on the debate stage. Having rural leaders involved when message, strategy, and funding decisions are made will transform the way our party deploys resources. There is no reason we cannot require at least one of the DNC officer positions be drawn from a Democratic leader living in a rural community. We can also elect the various committee positions in our party, like those responsible for the platform and rules that govern the presidential nomination, by regions—South, West, Midwest, and East—to give better geographic diversity of opinion and ideas running our national party. While this solution might not be perfect and the larger states in the regions can outnumber the smaller ones, this at least gives more rural states a chance at leadership. At this point the posts are all selected by the chair of the DNC. Dr. James Zogby, founder of the Arab American Institute, served on the DNC for over twenty-five years. He told me in the past, "DNC members were seen as props in meetings rather than decision-makers at the table." While we made some major reforms with the Unity and Reform Commission, we still have a long way to go to make the DNC more transparent and accountable.

Unless you live in a red and rural state, you can look at the voter registration numbers and think investing in certain races is a hopeless case. But I live in a red and rural state. I can tell you about races we can win that would never come up on the radar unless you come from rural. Not only do we have towns that are now 25 to 70 percent Latino, we have towns that are old-school Democratic, with strong Irish, Polish, and Czech immigrant families who have been in Nebraska for generations and consistently vote for Democrats. The problem is, they, too, have begun to feel like their vote does not matter because no one is investing in the rural candidates. Putting more rural Democrats in leadership roles will help bridge the knowledge gap in our party. Rural leaders know what races are possible to win that on paper look impossible. We now know our teams are stronger with more women and communities of color. The same is true for rural voices. I am telling you, there are races to be won in rural communities and states. We need to listen to rural leaders and grassroots activists, which means giving them leadership roles so they are included when the decisions are made. When we stop flying over rural and red states and start investing real money in the leaders and candidates, we will transform the political landscape.

REFORM THE ELECTORAL COLLEGE AND OPEN THE PRIMARIES

The rules of the road for our elections are outdated. When you have a person winning the electoral college and not the popular vote, you have to start looking at possible necessary reforms. Nebraska and Maine are the only two states to split their electoral votes, which means we are not winner-take-all states. This system enables voters in the different congressional districts to have their voices heard. It is not a perfect system, given all the gerrymandering that has taken place at the hands of Republicans, but it is better than the status quo and certainly better than getting rid of the electoral college altogether. I understand the allure of saying our presidential elections should be based on the popular vote. If this happens, rural states will never see a presidential candidate and the issues that impact our lives will never even be considered. If a candidate could go to Brooklyn and get in front of more voters than in, say, Alaska, North Dakota, Vermont, and Wyoming combined, guess where that candidate is going to go. This is not good on many levels. For one, we still have the United States Senate, where we need to win elections, and if our top-of-the-ticket candidates ignore these states, the resources will also never show up. We first need to end gerrymandering to ensure that congressional districts reflect the voters' partisan backgrounds. We then need to reform the Electoral College, where congressional districts give their votes based on the outcome in each district.

One other way to bring reform to our elections is to open our primaries and welcome Independent voters.

Right now, the fastest-growing "party" across the country is Independent. In red states, Democrats simply will not win elections without the majority of Independents voting for our candidates. The best way to build a relationship with Independent voters and earn their votes is to respect them enough to open the ballot in the primary for them to vote for Democratic candidates.

As chair of the Nebraska Democratic Party, I led an initiative to move from a caucus, in which we required voters to be Democrats to participate in choosing a presidential candidate, to an open primary, where we allow and welcome Independents to vote in the presidential primary. I truly love the organizing possibilities a caucus brings to a state. However, for our state, which does not get a lot of outside resources, they were an expensive process that got even more expensive with the new reforms the DNC put in place to make them more accessible after the 2016 cycle. I was part of the Unity and Reform Commission that developed these new policies. It made much more sense for our state to move to an open primary in order to help us win more elections. If an Independent voter—or any voter, for that matter—votes for a candidate in the primary election, he or she is more likely to vote for the candidate in the general election. Inviting Independents to vote with us, while not requiring them to become Democrats, allows those voters to be true to their values of independence and allows Democrats to win elections with a strong base of voters. This is a win-win for the Democratic Party and our body politic.

Of course I hope that Independent voters will see how welcoming the Democratic Party is and might consider joining our party officially. This is especially true for new Americans, the increasing number of immigrants becoming citizens across the country, with large numbers in the Midwest. Political refugees from Sudan, Iraq, Somalia, Togo, and many other countries are choosing to live in the Midwest because of the safe, small towns, the low cost of living, and access to good-paying jobs. When I was registering voters with a local nonprofit, Heartland Workers Center, a voter asked about the difference between Democrats and Republicans. When I started to explain the different platforms, one of the other volunteers from the community, Sergio Sosa, a political refugee himself, said simply, "Obama is a Democrat and Trump is a Republican." Point made.

We take for granted that potential voters know the difference between the parties. Many people do not and look at politics as complicated. It is our job to welcome voters into the Democratic Party, making the case for them to be proud Democrats. Research tells us if a voter votes with a party three times in a row, they become a party voter for life. I want Independents, new Americans, and young people voting with us, making our party stronger and giving us the ability to win elections in unexpected places.

BUILD A BRIDGE, LOCALLY

We do not need to wait for anyone to show up in our towns to start building a bridge between urban and rural Democrats. If you are an elected official from an urban area, work with a rural official to write a bill together. Maybe it'll be on expanding hemp production or requiring a certain percentage of food in our public institutions of schools, hospitals, and prisons to come from local family farmers and ranchers. Or beyond lawmaking, you can team up with a fellow Democrat living in a rural town to help canvass for a rural candidate. I watched an urban donor, Katie Weitz, bring rural candidates to Omaha so they could explain to other donors the issues critically important to rural people and their plans for when they were elected. This was great for the candidates, who got access to donors they would have never been able to reach, and great for urban Democrats, who do not hear enough from rural candidates on the unique challenges they face and the issues they are running on in small towns.

I often joke with my friends that everyone is falling over themselves to eat and drink locally. Which of course is great—I want more and more people honoring family farmers and ranchers along with those who brew craft beer or make local wine rather than buying items from big-box stores. This theory and love of local seems to go out the window on politics and voting. We need to be just as obsessed about finding the best rural candidate in our state as we are about searching for the best craft beer. Every state has candidates running in rural towns. Nebraska had over 850 Democrats run in 2018. Yes, 850. Most of the candidates were in rural parts of our state. Over 73 percent of the candidates won their elections. We did not win any of the federal or statewide races, but we elected state senators, mayors, city council members, university regents, school board members, natural resources board members, and boards of directors for public power companies. These Democrats are now in positions that have a real influence—building up local utilities, keeping university tuition costs down, adding more sources of clean energy, and ensuring that our schools are inclusive.

You have the power to build your own bridge to help break down the urban and rural divide. Get involved in your county and state Democratic Party, where rural and urban grassroots individuals are all working together to win elections. Even if at first it might not seem to make sense with the way meetings are facilitated (yes, *Robert's Rules of Order* does get bandied about a lot), the party needs more voices and more people at the table who care about building bridges. We need more younger voices in the party standing with the old-timers and learning from one another about ways to reach rural voters, from old-school techniques of calling and going to where the voters are—sale barns, coffee shops, and parades—to new methods like texting and social media. The party structures will always be there to help elect Democrats. It's up to us to make sure the party is strong. Do not re-create the wheel starting another new group. Bring your grit and creativity to the party.

SMASHING THE RURAL STEREOTYPES AND WINNING AGAIN

Matt Hildreth, with the group RuralOrganizing.org, is constantly doing polling and on-the-ground training to advocate for more groups and candidates to focus on rural people. Matt sees the possibility to win back rural voters, and it starts by smashing these three stereotypes. Matt reminds us all what is at stake. "In American politics geography matters. With the Senate and the Electoral College, the United States' political system gives rural voters more say than urban ones. Republicans know this and have spent the last four decades consolidating rural voters instead of running on a popular vote strategy." We need to reach rural voters to win again.

1. REJECT RURAL STEREOTYPES.

"Rural" is an identity just as much as a geography. The truth is, rural voters—who often identify themselves as moderate or conservative ideologically—tend to support pro-working-class

Democratic policies. Democrats and progressives too often fail to recognize this. Without a doubt, rural voters lean right.

According to polling conducted by RuralOrganizing .org in the weeks leading up to the 2018 midterm elections, two-thirds of rural residents (68 percent) consider themselves to be conservative or moderate, over 50 percent (52 percent) approve of Donald Trump's job performance, and when it came to generic House candidates in 2018, Republicans held a ten-point margin (43–33).

However, polling also strongly suggests that small-town voters feel the system is rigged for the powerful and wealthy, and a clear majority (77 percent) of rural residents think Congress is giving tax breaks to the wealthy instead of investing in rural areas.

Over 75 percent think politicians blame new immigrants or people of color to divide and distract from the real source of our problems instead of delivering for working people.

Two out of three (67 percent) support offering free tuition to local community colleges and trade schools, and a similar number (64 percent) want Medicare to cover all Americans. Over half (54 percent) back an increase of the minimum wage to $15 an hour, and only 38 percent support outlawing abortions.

But despite the popularity of progressive policies among small-town voters, a majority of rural

Americans (55 percent) don't think Democrats are fighting for their community.

In order to win again in rural communities, Democrats should embrace messages that reject big money in politics, call out racist strategies of division, expand access to programs like Medicare and Medicaid, and favor small, local businesses over major corporations.

2. INVEST IN RURAL COMMUNITIES OF COLOR.

Since the election of Donald Trump, many pundits and professional Democrats have "white washed" rural America. But the fact is, immigrants are revitalizing small towns and rural communities across the country, while African American voters across the rural South and Native Americans in the Great Plains have long been critical members of the Democratic coalition.

Roughly one in five (19 percent) rural residents in the United States are people of color.

Republicans understand that rural voters of color are critical to deciding control of the House. That's why they target voter suppression efforts on indigenous voters in North Dakota, Latinos in southwest Kansas, and black voters across the rural south.

Democrats must understand that the demographics of rural communities are not homogeneous. It's critical to invest in rural communities of color and engage these voters with authentic policy solutions to the unique challenges they face.

3. PROVIDE RURAL-SPECIFIC SOLUTIONS TO RURAL-SPECIFIC PROBLEMS.

Recent polling shows rural Americans are deeply concerned about fighting for small-town ways of life. Nearly every participant (94 percent) in our polling said rural and small-town ways of life is worth fighting for.

Furthermore, 90 percent of rural Americans think we should invest in small, local businesses and protect rural schools from closing, and 85 percent think we should protect hunting and fishing habitats through smart land management policies. Similarly, 80 percent of rural Americans want to pass policies that support rural grocery stores, pharmacies, and clinics, and three out of four rural residents want individuals with drug addictions sent to rehabilitation centers instead of prisons.

Rural Americans want rural-specific solutions to rural-specific problems, and the policies they support come straight from the progressive platform. Democrats should lean into them.

EPILOGUE: CLOSING THE GATE

When you arrive at a ranch, you close the gate behind you to ensure the cattle do not go roaming off. That act is a sign you care about the other people around you and you care about the critters. It's a simple act, but one that also requires action and thought. Winning back rural voters is also a simple act and requires the actions and thoughts of the entire Democratic Party.

One of rural Democrats' most effective leaders and advocates recently passed away. Frank LaMere, Manape Huk ga "Soldier Chief," made his journey home to the Creator while I wrote this book. He had a rare form of cancer that impacts Native Americans six times more than that of other populations. Frank is forever part of my heart. Frank started the Native American Caucus at the national level years ago when just two DNC members represented tribal nations. He was the longest-serving Native American on the DNC. Frank was a warrior for justice. He ended the illegal selling of beer in Whiteclay, where a store was selling millions of cans of alcohol a year in a town with a population of twelve. When I was first deciding to run for chair of the Nebraska Democratic

Party, I started to question if I should run. Who was I to come in and run right out of the gate for chair? Maybe I should run for vice chair? I was listening to others in the party saying I shouldn't do it, that I was too much of an "activist" to serve as a party leader and that maybe I should learn the ropes of the internal state party operations before I decide to run. Frank heard I was maybe thinking about not running or putting myself up for vice chair instead. I vividly remember the call he made to me. Frank does not get upset often, so when he does, you stand up and listen. "Jane, this Frank LaMere. You do not take the back seat to anyone. You have put in the time. You have collected the road dust. You are ready for this moment. You must not give your power over to anyone. When no one stood up for Mother Earth, you did. You looked the powerful in the eye and did not back down. You must run and I want to run with you as your vice chair. Together. I will put tobacco down as you reflect on this." We did run together, and we won.

There were plenty of naysayers who thought Frank and I would lead too much like "activists" and would not be able to separate from the grassroots issues we both deeply care about to govern the party effectively. Frank and I both led our entire lives with one foot in the streets and one foot in party politics. It is precisely because of this we are effective leaders. Frank always stood with those who need second chances. He never judged someone based on where they lived, but rather on what they lived for. Frank always saw the work ahead of us and invited everyone to the table. He believed no other party can lift people up like the Democrats. "There is work to be done," Frank would always tell me. We stand proud as Democrats no matter where we live, never compromising our values and always making the case to voters face to face, shoulder to shoulder.

The beauty of the Democratic Party has always been our diversity—of race, of gender, of religion, of sexual orientation, of geography. We are a big-tent party. We accept people of different backgrounds. We have always prided ourselves on the fact that the diversity in our party produces a diversity of ideas and therefore better policies. As Speaker Nancy Pelosi says, "Diversity is our strength, unity is our power." Right now we have a division between the progressive and the moderate wings of our party. We need to fix that so we can pull together to win elections and put in place elected officials who care about our families. You need both wings to fly, as Larry Cohen, a union leader and chair of Our Revolution, always reminds me. When we have setbacks, like we recently did when we tried to secure a DNC climate debate, Larry usually gives me a big smile and says, "Forward ever." He has more battle scars inside the party trying to get a more fair and representative party of the people than most leaders I know. Fifteen years later, he is still pushing the DNC to reform. Forward ever.

A big tent comes with loud, rowdy voices often at odds with one another, and those conversations—and sometimes fights—are what usually creates the best outcomes. When we have all shades of blue at the table, we are better off. We should not be purposefully fomenting another division, that between urban and rural, as we bring different ideas forward. Ultimately, there is more that unites us than divides us.

I THINK A LOT ABOUT FRANK'S WORDS: THERE IS WORK TO BE DONE. ONE OF the biggest problems Democrats have in rural America is one of trust—a belief we will actually follow through with the words spoken in speeches and rallies. There is a real doubt out in the farms and fields of our country that Democrats, no matter what they might say, are actually concerned about the interests of rural families. Rural people are largely invisible to the vast majority of the Democratic Party. Even worse, rural families know they are seen by Democrats as part of the reason why Trump got elected in the first place. They are afraid the Democratic Party has simply stopped thinking about them entirely. It is easy for Democrats to write off rural voters. It is much harder to reach out, listen, and learn from rural people on how we can make our party stronger.

Let's do this work. Let's come together and push back against the common threats to all our communities, both urban and rural. Without question, we have our differences, both on the cultural level as well as on issues like abortion and gun reform. And yet when I sit in a diner in the ranch country of Nebraska's Sandhills or in a diner in the urban center of North Omaha, I hear worried conversations about the same things: their kid's school lacking the funding it needs to pay teachers or even do basic maintenance; the rising costs of college and insurance; a shortage of jobs with a living wage; unsustainable costs for rent or housing; and at every turn, big corporations bent on proving they have more power than we the people. Because both rural and urban residents want these things to change, this is a bridge we can build. Get out there and collect some road dust on your car. There's work to be done.

#HarvestTheVote

SOME THINGS YOU SHOULD KNOW WHEN YOU VISIT RURAL AMERICA

Now that you are ready to connect and stand with rural communities across America to build power together for our families, let me leave you with a few last words.

I am including both a glossary of sayings and other tips for urban folks so you don't make the same mistakes I did—although it is okay to make mistakes, too; it's how we learn and laugh with one another to build relationships . . . you're welcome ahead of time.

I end the book with a list of organizations working every day in rural towns that could use your support as well as some reading and listening you can do to keep learning about rural America.

Never ask how many cattle someone owns or how much land they own.

When you do this, you are essentially asking how much money a person has in his or her bank account. A rancher might be polite and answer, but you will probably get some variation of "We have enough grass for the cows and enough cows for the grass."

Wave when a car passes you on the two-lane road (mostly gravel and dirt roads).

Some prefer a full flip of the entire hand. Most of the old-timers keep their hands on the wheel and just

lift a finger. Not that finger. The pointer finger. You
should always do it. Be nice. It will make you smile.

Supper is dinner. Dinner is lunch.

Rural folks eat their noon meal and call it dinner. The
evening meal is supper. Get it right and don't be late.

**Most gas stations in rural towns are also the grocery store
and the gallery for local art. They are also where old-timers
have coffee.**

Walk in and say hello or give a nod. Buy some of the
local pottery. You might have to pump your gas and
then come in and tell the shopkeeper how much you
pumped. We trust people.

**If you park your car on someone's farm or ranch, leave your
keys on the dashboard.**

Your car might have to be moved in order to get
a tractor out or to perform some other chore. We
promise we won't steal your car.

Respect the land.

Most work their entire lives to own a piece of land.
Or the land has been passed down through the
generations. Don't make comments about some of the
outbuildings. The person's great-grandpa probably
built it with his own hands.

**GPS may not work in rural communities. Ask for directions.
Be prepared to listen.**

Directions will be something like this: "Turn right
on the oil road, go east three miles, turn north
by the red barn, and watch out for deer." *Definitely*
watch out for deer. You can make hash out of them
and they can total your car. Also, an oil road is how
old-timers describe a paved road. I once looked for
a street sign that said "oil road." I was lost for an

hour until the rancher came and found me. He was laughing.

Close the gate behind you.

When you have to open a gate to enter the next section of someone's farm or ranch, you need to close the gate behind you. Super critical. Otherwise cows or other critters they are raising will get out. Chasing down a cow that wanders off is no fun for anyone.

If you get stuck, ask for help.

I have been stuck in snowstorms and on muddy shoulders and have had flat tires all in the middle of "nowhere." Every single time a local farmer, rancher, or town sheriff came to my rescue. Sometimes it involved my walking up to the closest ranch and other times I simply stopped on the side of the road and folks immediately stopped to help. The great thing about small towns is people want to help each other. You might even leave with a dozen fresh eggs or some pretty good life lessons from an old-timer.

Sale barns have good cafés, but you will not find clothes.

Sale barns are where people in the community bring their livestock for auction. They usually have a really yummy café that makes the best grilled ham and cheese and fried chicken. You can sit in and watch the auctions. Always fun. Especially if the local 4-H club is selling cattle that day—nothing like the face of an eight-year-old who's selling her first calf.

Speaking of clothes: forget about the mall or Target. Farm stores are where it's at.

Farm stores like Orscheln Farm & Home sell Wranglers for $20 (a bit lower than Free People and Urban Outfitters). The same plaid shirt I have seen in Urban Outfitters for $100, you can find at Orschelns for $25. Yes, you can get a Carhartt jacket also. Really, you can get just about anything for yourself, the cows, or your dog.

Branding is not an exercise for a communications plan.
Ranch families still get together and help each other brand the calves and give them shots. Animal cruelty? No. I promise you. The calf is down for maybe a minute and they get right back up and usually run right to their mama. It's all okay. It's not harsh. It's how we track cattle. The food is always amazing. Don't fall for the "Oysters" trick. Unless you want to try fresh or breaded bull balls. Rocky Mountain Oysters are breaded testicles, not some midwest twist on Oysters Rockefeller. Oh, and "Calf Fries" are the same thing, just smaller.

GROUPS YOU CAN SUPPORT

The best way you can be part of rebuilding the Democratic Party with rural voters at the table is to come out and connect with the land and support groups who do this work every day. It's going to take a lot of work and we are all going to have to collect a lot of road dust to get this done. Good news is, you get to see beautiful, vast, quirky, and diverse rural communities while you stand with us (and eat really good, locally grown food!). A portion of all book sales will go to support these groups who love and work in rural America. I deeply believe in the power of organizing, lifting up rural voices, and electing more rural Democrats. These groups are part of the solution.

Association of State Democratic Committees, asdc.democrats.org

The best place to invest in red and rural states in order to build up the infrastructure to win elections for Democrats is to give money to state and county parties. You can find your state party and donate directly to them. When you are on the state party website, look up your local/county party also. They need your help, too. The single best thing you can do to help elect Democrats up and down the ballot is to invest in your state and county party.

Bold Alliance, boldalliance.org

Bold started in Nebraska to help stop the Keystone XL Pipeline with the unlikely alliance of farmers, ranchers, environmentalists, and tribal nations. Bold now helps rural groups across the country push back on Big Oil and Big Ag threatening the land and water. Bold also works to elect more candidates representing rural communities and rural issues.

Family Farm Action, farmaction.us

A coalition of family farmers and advocates building the political muscle to fight for farmers and rural communities. Family Farm Action protects America's family farms and rural communities from multinational agribusiness monopolies that are destroying rural economies and our way of life.

Farm Aid, farmaid.org

Started by Willie Nelson, Neil Young, John Mellencamp, and later Dave Matthews, the yearly concert does not stop at an awesome rock show. Farm Aid helps family farmers and ranchers year-round with a suicide hotline, grants to continue their operations, and advocacy to have their voices heard in state legislatures and on Capitol Hill. While Farm Aid is not a partisan group, they are the one group who every year celebrates rural voices with a platform bigger than any other.

RuralOrganizing.org, ruralorganizing.org

A group of over 50,000 rural activists staying connected to rebuild rural America. They conduct polling and research, and they advocate to include rural issues in national politics. Their mission is rooted in the simple belief that local people know how to solve local problems.

MORE READING

I find many books about rural America are filled with sadness, addiction, and hopelessness. I hope these books and podcasts give a different view of the people, the land, and the way of life in rural towns.

Cather, Willa. *My Ántonia*

Immigrants from all over the world came to the Great Plains. This beautifully written story follows a Bohemian family. The way Willa describes the land resonates still to this day.

Clyburn, James E. *Blessed Experiences: Genuinely Southern, Proudly Black*

Representative Clyburn's stories of the small towns and growing up black in the South are rooted in history as he describes his path to Majority Whip. (University of South Carolina Press, 2015)

Foxfire Fund, *The Foxfire Book of Simple Living: Celebrating Fifty Years of Listenin', Laughin', and Learnin'*

No one thought a book series about how to hunt, make moonshine, build a log cabin, and engage in faith healing would be bestsellers, but they were! The books shaped generations on how they viewed rural. (Anchor, 2016)

Horton, Myles, and Paulo Freire. *We Make the Road by Walking: Conversations on Education and Social Change*
A book about social change through a lens of literacy and poverty programs happening in rural communities. (Temple University Press, 1990)

Genoways, Ted. *This Blessed Earth: A Year in the Life of an American Family Farm*
The story of the Hammond family: how they confront the changing landscape and threats to family farmers. (W. W. Norton, 2018)

Hewitt, Ben. *The Town That Food Saved: How One Community Found Vitality in Local Food*
A town of 300 people transformed jobs, the economy, and its self-image with food. (Rodale, 2011)

Hightower, Jim. *Thieves in High Places: They've Stolen Our Country—And It's Time to Take It Back*
Anything Jim writes will make you laugh and think. This is one of his many books about how the grass roots can take back our politics. (Viking, 2003)

Nagle, Rebecca. *This Land* (podcast)
The podcast follows how a murder in Oklahoma set up a case in front of the Supreme Court that will determine the fate of tribal nations and half the land in the state. The podcast is published

by Crooked Media, who also puts out Pod Save America. All of their podcasts are must-listens to stay grounded in hope and to stay connected to strategic political thinking. (2019)

Pipher, Mary. *The Middle of Everywhere: Helping Refugees Enter the American Community*

Mary tells the stories of refugees building the American Dream. Rural towns and cities are embracing refugees and immigrants, and Mary reminds us why they make our country better. (Mariner, 2003)

Vaughan, Carson. *Zoo Nebraska: The Dismantling of an American Dream*

A story about a quirky rural town, with residents' backstories and the big personalities we find in just about every small town. (Little A, 2019)

ACKNOWLEDGMENTS

Throughout the book, I tell stories of moments and people that I do not list again here. Instead, I share my love for people I could not include in the book but who influence my thinking and who challenge me to be a better leader. With the one exception of my family, I include them again!

Scott, Kora, Maya, and Willa, who share my time with the entire state of Nebraska. Scott never bores on the latest inside-baseball issue I want to talk about when I get home late. Our girls have put up with a mom whose trunk is often filled with yard signs and who runs into their school events a little late but who does this work to make the world better for them. Mamma loves you.

Mom, Abby, Rich, and Sean, who still call me childhood nicknames even though I am forty-six. Each of you shaped who I am today. The fights in the pool and endless games of hide-and-go-seek prepared me to take on people bigger than me. And Abby, my sister who proudly wears her heart on her sleeve, I am still not sitting down. I am still at my desk busy making things.

Adam, Bianca, Logan, Noah, Preston, and Peyton, I

am lucky to be your aunt. No matter what, keep traveling and meeting new people who think differently than you.

JoAnn and Al, Scott's parents, who have stepped in to watch the girls when Scott and I were both on the road. I am so thankful for your red pen, Al, and you passing down cooking tips, JoAnn. The amount of time you dedicate to our family means everything to me.

Donnie, my best friend and Kora's godfather, who would have guessed our street activism all those years ago would lead us to follow our hearts and marry guys who love rural towns? Thank you for loving the girls as if they were your own.

Paul and Marsha, who gave me my first job in partisan politics and pulled me aside, letting me know if I only protested in the streets and did not also get people elected who shared my values, I was not truly impacting long-term change.

Zack, who heard me on The Wilderness podcast and sent me a direct message on Twitter asking if I ever thought about writing a book. Well, here it is. This would have never happened without you. I am pretty lucky you love politics as much as you love crime fiction.

SNT, otherwise known as Senator Nina Turner, who in turn calls me JFK (Jane Fleming Kleeb). SNT says "any blue won't do" and I say "all shades of blue" while we both push for the same goal—working families represented at all levels of government. I respect your strength, love, and ability to outwork any guy that comes into your path. I always have your back.

The Nebraska Democratic Party officers and staff— Patty, Richard, Preston, Ron, Charlene, Ted, Jim, Precious, Kevin, Ron, Jessica, and Gina. I am honored to stand shoulder to shoulder with you on a daily basis to transform the political landscape of our state.

The constant Bold staffer, Mark, who writes the blogs, takes the video, creates the strategy, and never stops working. Thank you for being my right hand and left hand. You are a rock.

Malinda, who joined the Bold team when it was only a concept on two pieces of paper. Thank you for believing in the vision. I hope to always remain your batman.

Tim, Barry, and Brian, who always knew I would be late to our lunch meetings. Thank you for loving my crazy ideas and for validating that my way of thinking about politics matters.

Stephanie, Spencer, Dulce, Brian, Joe, Jason, and Mechelle, who push me to make our party inclusive and welcoming. Each of you has truly changed the face of our party.

Shannon, Lori, Bonnie, Susan, Diana, Jeanne, Suz, Nancy, Sue, Amy—the women of the pipeline fight. The ones who make cookies, sew quilts (even one for Obama!), work cattle, and raise hell. You are the reason I fight every day.

Ben, Graham, Bob, Earl, Mason, and Thunderpants (the pipeline-fighting pony), you were the cowboys of the fight never scared to ride a horse through the streets of Washington, D.C., or to tell TransCanada and politicians right to their face they were wrong.

The photographers and artists of the pipeline fight—Justin, Steve, John, Alex, Mary Anne, Rick, and Mike. Thank you for your creativity and heart while bringing lots of crazy ideas to life—including crop arts, armbands, yard signs, concerts in cornfields, albums recorded in the solar barn, and tipis that now sit in the Smithsonian.

My pipeline-fighting sister Joye, who, like me, has been told she is a loudmouth once or twice. Joye was one of the first people to fight the KXL Pipeline and one of the first women to create a camp at Standing Rock. Thank you for leading when no one else is looking.

Dallas, the funniest water protector I know, thank you for using your gift of humor to bring serious issues to the forefront. I have learned how to be a better ally from you, Dallas. Thank you for pushing me.

Daryl, Annie, and Shailene, who showed me what strong, quiet leadership looks like. Most will never know all that you have done to impact the KXL and Standing Rock fights. I do and I am grateful.

Kyle, the Sandhills Boot guy, who makes the boots I proudly wear every day to kick some ass. Thank you for works of art that both inspire me and keep me grounded. I need new soles again. Sorry!

Jen and Ken—the legal eagles of the pipeline fight. You kept us in the fight when others thought we hit a dead end. We are all forever grateful for the years you have each committed to representing us in the courts.

Mike, Gene, Jamie, Kendall, Anthony, Lena, Tiernan, Erich, Kate, Josh, Susan, Liz, Beth, and all the members of the "big greens" who welcomed the unlikely alliance and rebel Bold pipeline fighters to the table and treated us as equal partners. Thank you for never giving up on us.

Tewes, the one person on this list I will only call by his last name. You broke the mold for "political consultants" and showed me the power of the inside game.

J.D. and every Democrat running in a rural district. You are creating the path for future Dems to follow. Proud to be part of the Dollar Store Dem Caucus with you, brother. Keep pushing the party to invest in rural.

The Townhouse Tavern and (former!) Young Dems Nomiki, Matt, Murshed, both Aris, Guy, Colin, Biko, Billy, Chris, Tony, Jay, Crystal, Dan, and Amber. We fought over candidates, drank beers, worked endless hours, and wrote plans . . . wait, we still are. Thank you for making politics fun.

To all the ASDC staff, my fellow DNC members and state party chairs—with special love to Trav, Martha, Tina, Joe, Betty, Vicki, Terje, Ben, Christine, Governor

Walters, and Jessica—and the #DirtRoadDems who collect road dust across our states and know our rural towns, I see you. I value the time you put in to show that rural people have solutions to the big problems facing our country. Here's to endless miles we drive to #HarvestTheVote.

INDEX

Index

Index

Index

Index